MARK TWAIN:

America's Humorist, Dreamer, Prophet

MARK TWAIN:

America's Humorist, Dreamer, Prophet

Clinton Cox

SCHOLASTIC INC.
New York Toronto London Auckland Sydney

Front cover photo: © *The Bettmann Archive*
Book designed by Elizabeth B. Parisi

ISBN 0-590-45641-5

12 11 10 9   4 5 6 7 8 9/0

Printed in the U.S.A.   40

First Scholastic printing, September 1998

CONTENTS

PROLOGUE

There have been few writers as riddled with contradictions as Mark Twain, or as powerfully shaped by the society they lived in.

The years between Twain's birth and death (1835–1910) were a time of profound social, political, and economic change that radically altered the lives of most people in the United States.

When he was born, the system of slavery that had existed since the time of the first English colonies was still firmly embedded in this country. The United States remained the agricultural society it had been since its founding and exerted little influence beyond its still-expanding borders.

By the time Twain was thirty years old, slavery had been ended by the Civil War with its hundreds of thousands of casualties, and the age of large-scale industrialization and capitalism had already begun to shift large numbers of people from the countryside to the burgeoning cities.

Changes within the United States were accompanied by a steady expansion of the country's influence outside its borders, and by the time Twain passed away at the age of seventy-five, the power of the United States had spread around the world.

Mark Twain voiced the hopes and dreams, the fears and confusions felt by millions of other Americans during those decades of turmoil and change.

His voice was their voice: a voice struggling to find itself in the midst of awesome ambiguities and contradictions.

He was the son of slaveowners, yet he wrote some of the most powerful antislavery literature of his day.

He bitterly denounced the capitalists who were building huge fortunes while, all around them, as Twain wrote, "hunger, persecution and death" were the wages of the poor. Yet he counted many of those same capitalists among his friends, and invested hundreds of thousands of dollars trying desperately to be rich himself.

He wrote such scathing attacks against churches and clergymen that he was often called the "son of the Devil."

"I cannot see how a man of any large degree of humorous perception can ever be religious — except he purposely shut the eyes of his mind & keep them shut by force," he said in his notebook.

Yet he also wrote that he believed in God, "the One who created this majestic universe and rules it. . . . His real character is written in plain words in

America's humorist, dreamer, prophet in his later years.

his real Bible, which is Nature and her history."

And always, no matter what other issues were fueling Twain's passions and driving his writings, he came back to the country's great unresolved issue of race: the struggle over the ultimate status of the black men, women, and children who were finally legally free, but still subjected to violence and inequality throughout the United States.

This racial conflict seemed to increasingly haunt him as he grew older, and even invaded his dreams.

Twain became a man obsessed by race, and by the injustices that racism spawned. In his later years he found time to speak at black churches, while telling white congregations he was too busy. And among other acts of generosity toward black people, he paid the expenses of several college students "as part of the reparation due from every white to every black man."

In "Which Is It?," his final long piece of fiction about the South, he expressed the anger not of the white race he belonged to, but of the black race he had once looked down upon.

In *The Adventures of Huckleberry Finn*, Twain had written about the escaping slave, Jim, and the white youth who helped him. Twain showed their common humanity and, in a book that has been called the genesis of American fiction, held out hope for an eventual reconciliation of the races in the United States.

In order to comfort himself and his suffering wife, Livy, on the night she died, he sang spirituals he'd heard slaves sing when he was a child. Twain's voice carried across the room, said his daughter Clara, with a sound that was "an emotional outcry, rather than a song."

His racial attitudes, like almost everything else about Mark Twain, both mirrored and magnified the world around him.

But probably the most striking thing about Twain — and a measure of his genius — was his ability to write humorously about issues that made him seethe with anger.

Twain believed that laughter was the "one really effective weapon" people possessed in their struggle against injustice.

"Power, money, persuasion, supplication, persecution — these can lift at a colossal humbug — push it a little, weaken it a little, century by century; but only laughter can blow it to rags and atoms at a blast," he wrote in *The Mysterious Stranger*. "Against the assault of laughter nothing can stand."

For almost fifty years, beginning as a young reporter covering the territorial legislature in Carson City, Nevada, Twain used the weapon of laughter to assault colossal humbugs wherever he found them.

His words can still make us laugh and, if we are open to what he called "the gravity which is the foundation, and of real value" underlying the words, they can still teach us much about ourselves and the world around us.

1

A HEAVENLY PLACE
FOR A BOY

The man the world would come to know as Mark
Twain was born Samuel Langhorne Clemens, on
November 30, 1835. His birthplace was a two-room
frame house in Florida, in Monroe County, Missouri,
an isolated place that consisted of two unpaved
streets, twenty-one houses, and one hundred people.

Twain was born two months ahead of schedule, as
Halley's Comet blazed through the sky.

"I increased the population by 1 per cent," he said.
"It is more than many of the best men in history
could have done for a town . . . and it shows that I
could have done it for any place — even London, I
suppose."

"Little Sam," as his family called him — was the
sixth living child of John and Jane Clemens (a boy
had died at the age of three months several years before).

His father was a lawyer, farmer, merchant, and
speculator who was always chasing dreams of
wealth that never materialized. He had recently
moved the family from Tennessee in yet another attempt to find prosperity.

In Florida, John Clemens ran a general store, worked on inventing a perpetual motion machine, and tried to convince Congress to fund the Salt River Navigation Project — a scheme to make the narrow Salt River navigable by large riverboats from the Mississippi, eighty-five miles to the east.

But Congress refused to fund the project, ending yet another of the elder Clemens's dreams. The perpetual motion machine never worked, of course, and the store did not do well.

John Clemens "had no luck" in Florida, his son wrote many years later, "except that I was born to him."

Birthplace of Samuel Langhorne Clemens (Mark Twain).

So once again Clemens moved his family, this time to the village his son would one day make famous: Hannibal, Missouri.

Little Sam was four years old when the family settled into a small house three blocks from what he would describe in *Life on the Mississippi* as "the great Mississippi, the magnificent Mississippi, rolling its mile-wide tide along."

His father opened a general store in Hannibal, a community that consisted of a few new brick houses scattered among several old log cabins, wooden houses, and vacant lots. North, south, and west of the village was a vast expanse of forest and prairie, with a few farms scattered here and there.

Little Sam was not close to his father, a man he said never demonstrated affection for anyone in the family, but he was very close to his mother.

"Her interest in people and other animals was warm, personal, friendly," he wrote years later. "She always found something to excuse, and as a rule to love, in the toughest of them — even if she had to put it there herself."

In addition to his mother and father, Sam lived in the crowded house with his brothers, Orion, Benjamin, and Henry, and his sisters, Pamela and Mary. Another sister, nine-year-old Margaret, had died shortly before the family left Florida. All except Henry were older than Sam.

Twain's mother, who once told him, "You gave me more trouble than any child I had."

His father also owned or rented slaves whenever he could afford to, and they usually slept on the kitchen floor.

Slavery, which would figure prominently in so much of Mark Twain's writings, especially *The Adventures of Huckleberry Finn*, was something he knew intimately during his childhood.

Decades after leaving Hannibal, he vividly remembered seeing a dozen black men and women chained together on Hannibal's lone wharf, waiting to be shipped downriver to the unspeakable brutality of plantation slavery in the Deep South.

Their faces, he said, were the saddest he had ever seen.

And one night when he was only four, Little Sam tossed and turned in his bed while listening to the groans of a captured runaway slave tied up in a nearby shack.

Beatings of slaves also occurred in the Clemenses' house. Once his mother was about to beat a young slave named Jenny with a cowhide whip, when Jenny snatched the whip from her hand. When Twain's father heard about the incident, he raced home, bound the young woman's wrists together and beat her.

His father often slapped a slave boy named Lewis because he was awkward. His father also sometimes beat Lewis with a whip, an act that terrified the slave.

Though he would later condemn both the institution of slavery and his father's involvement in it, Twain said that as a child " . . . I was not aware that there was anything wrong about it. No one arraigned it in my hearing; the local papers said nothing against it; the local pulpit taught us that God approved it, that it was a holy thing, and that the doubter need only look to the Bible. . . . "

Slave auctions were announced in the local newspapers and churches, and advertised on church bulletin boards. Once when a Methodist minister sold a little girl to another minister, and the new owner forced the child onto a steamboat, her mother stood screaming on the shore.

When Sam was five, his father was foreman of a

jury at the trial of three white abolitionists charged with helping five slaves escape to freedom. Many residents of Hannibal wanted to hang the abolitionists and, with his father leading the deliberations, the men were found guilty. There was widespread approval when each one was sentenced to twelve years at hard labor.

When Sam saw a white overseer kill a slave in Hannibal over a task awkwardly done, he knew the overseer had a legal right to kill the slave. But he also knew, in spite of everything he had been taught to the contrary, that what the overseer did was wrong.

There were no public schools in Missouri at the time, but Hannibal boasted two private schools, and Sam was sent to one taught by a Mrs. Horr.

She opened school with prayer, a chapter from the New Testament and an explanation of the chapter. One day she said that anyone who prayed for something earnestly and strongly would receive whatever it was they prayed for.

"I was so forcibly struck by this information and so gratified by the opportunities which it offered," Twain wrote in his *Autobiography*.

"I prayed for gingerbread. Margaret Kooneman, who was the baker's daughter, brought a slab of gingerbread to school every morning, she had always kept it out of sight before but when I finished my

*The town that Twain, "The Man From Hannibal,"
made famous.*

prayer and glanced up, there it was in easy reach
and she was looking the other way. In all my life I
believe I never enjoyed an answer to prayer more
than I enjoyed that one; and I was a convert, too."

He quickly became an ex-convert, however, when
his subsequent prayers for gingerbread went unan-
swered.

"I found that not even the most powerful prayer
was competent to lift that gingerbread again," he
said.

The prayer episode may not have had anything to
do with it, but Sam grew to hate going to school. He

was a frail child and was often able to stay home because of illness. Once, when an epidemic of measles was ravaging Hannibal, he climbed into bed with an infected friend in what turned out to be a successful effort to catch the disease.

"The family doctor . . . saved my life several times," he said later. "Still, he was a good man and meant well."

In one of their last conversations, his mother told him: "You gave me more trouble than any child I had."

"Afraid I wouldn't live?" he asked.

"No," his mother replied. "Afraid you would."

Summers were spent on the farm of his uncle John Quarles, who was married to his mother's youngest sister. The farm, which was four miles from Florida, was a fascinating place of woods and prairie that offered a welcome respite for both mother and child. "It was a heavenly place for a boy," Sam would remember.

For three months, he could enjoy himself, and his mother could rest while other people worried about what he was up to.

John Quarles also owned about a dozen slaves, all but one or two of them members of the same family, and Sam spent much of his time with them.

"All the negroes were friends of ours," he said, "and with those of our own age we were . . . comrades, and yet not comrades; color and condition interposed a subtle line which both parties were conscious of and which rendered fusion impossible."

It was on his Uncle John's farm that Sam learned many of the African-American stories and folklore that would become such an important part of *Huckleberry Finn* and other stories.

One of his most powerful memories of those summers was of "Uncle Daniel," the head of the slave family.

It was from this middle-aged black man that Sam first heard "The Golden Arm," a ghost story he later made famous by telling it to audiences around the world.

"I can see the white and black children grouped on the hearth . . . ," he recalled. "We would huddle close about the old man, & begin to shudder . . . & under the spell of his impressive delivery we always fell prey to that climax at the end when the rigid black shape in the twilight sprang at us with a shout."

Daniel also possessed the patience, friendliness, and loyalty Twain would attribute over forty years later to the escaping slave, Jim, in *Huckleberry Finn*.

Summers always ended too quickly for Sam, and the school year would once again find him playing hooky with his friends and finding new ways to get into trouble.

One of their favorite pastimes was exploring a huge cave three miles south of Hannibal.

Decades later, Twain would make both the cave and "Injun Joe" famous in *The Adventures of Tom Sawyer*. (In *Tom Sawyer*, Injun Joe was a thief and murderer who found a hoard of outlaw gold in a cave. The treasure was eventually given to Tom and Huck.)

Mrs. Horr taught only the first two or three grades, so when Sam grew older, he was enrolled in a school run by Mr. J.D. Dawson. There were approximately twenty-five pupils in the school, ranging in age from seven to a man in his twenties. It was in Dawson's school that Sam met the first Jews he or most of his classmates had ever seen: the Levin boys.

Jews were routinely condemned in the churches of Hannibal, and the local newspaper ran frequent articles charging Jewish merchants with cheating their customers. The reaction of Sam and his classmates to the Levin boys was, therefore, predictably negative. Sam's anti-Jewish feelings, like his anti-black feelings, were something he would later struggle against and largely overcome.

Dawson's school was also where young Sam first fell in love. Unfortunately for him, the girls he fell in love with were usually much older, and totally uninterested in his affections.

When he was nine, he fell in love with eighteen-year-old Mary Miller, who "was the first one that furnished me with a broken heart . . . she scorned me and I recognized that this was a cold world. I had not noticed that temperature before."

Another of his girlfriends was Laura Hawkins, who lived across the street from the Clemenses and was two years younger than Sam. Her name would appear in Twain's *The Gilded Age* and her character would be used as the model for Becky Thatcher, the blue-eyed girl Tom Sawyer fell in love with in *The Adventures of Tom Sawyer*.

Sam's adventures with his friends were far more thrilling than his romances, however.

Benson Blankenship, the older brother of Sam's friend, Tom, used to hunt and fish in the marshes on the Illinois side of the Mississippi. (Twain said that Tom Blankenship was the model for Huckleberry Finn.)

One day Benson found a runaway slave hiding in the swamps. The law made it a crime not to turn in slaves caught trying to escape to freedom, and there was a reward of $50 for this one. In addition, betraying the slave would have brought Benson the admiration of the town's leading citizens.

Benson was one of the poorest boys in Hannibal, but instead of turning in the slave, he brought him scraps of food for several weeks. Word of what was happening leaked out, though, and a gang of woodcutters chased the fleeing man into a swamp called Bird Slough, where he drowned.

A few days later, Sam and some friends went to

the spot and were pushing a pile of driftwood around. Suddenly the drowned man's body, disturbed by their pushing of the pile, rose up from the water. He had drowned feet first, and the top half of his body stood straight before them, his eyes seemingly staring at them.

The boys fled in terror, expecting to be grabbed by the dead man at every step. Benson's friendship with the escaping slave would form the basis for Huck Finn's friendship with Jim, another escaping slave, almost forty years later.

Sam seemed to have a knack for adventures.

One day several months later, he and a friend played hooky outside the town, and were unaware that a man had been stabbed in Hannibal as a result of an old family feud.

Onlookers carried the victim into an office used by Sam's father, where the man died and was left on the floor to be attended to in the morning.

When Sam grew tired of playing hooky, he decided to spend the night in the office, rather than risk his mother's anger. It was dark when he crept in and lay down on a sofa.

Gradually he became aware of a shape on the floor, but couldn't tell what it was. Then moonlight shining through a window suddenly revealed the dead man's face and the gaping wound in his chest.

"I went out of there," Twain remembered almost a lifetime later. "I do not say that I went away in any

Mark Twain, at the age of 15.

sort of a hurry, but I simply went; that is sufficient. I went out of the window, and I carried the sash along with me. I did not need the sash, but it was handier to take it than to leave it, and so I took it. I was not scared, but I was considerably agitated."

Few days seem to have been uneventful for Sam or his friends, but no matter what other adventures they were involved in, the center of their young lives was always the river.

They enjoyed it year-round: skating and sledding in the winter; boating, fishing, and swimming in the summer; and exploring the mysteries of the river-banks every season of the year.

Most of all, however, the river served as the place that made them dream of the world beyond Hanni-bal — a world that, in their eyes, was filled with wonders and adventures they couldn't even begin to imagine.

"Once a day a cheap, gaudy packet arrived upward from St. Louis, and another downward from Keokuk," Twain wrote. "Before these events, the day was glorious with expectancy; after them, the day was a dead and empty thing. Not only the boys, but the whole village, felt this."

A black man famous for his keen eyesight and booming voice would watch for the dark smoke from the boats and, as soon as he spotted it, cry: "S-t-e-a-m-boat a-comin'!"

Instantly, said Twain, "the dead town is alive and

moving. Drays, carts, men, boys, all go hurrying from many quarters to a common center, the wharf. Assembled there, the people fasten their eyes upon the coming boat as upon a wonder they are seeing for the first time."

The steamer was a long boat with two tall chimneys, a big glass pilothouse, and decks crowded with passengers.

Once the boat docked, "such a scramble as there is to get aboard, and to get ashore, and to take in freight and to discharge freight, all at one and the same time; and such a yelling and cursing as the mates facilitate it all with! Ten minutes later the steamer is under way again. . . . After ten more minutes the town is dead again. . . . "

Sam and the other boys had many passing ambitions, but only one permanent ambition — to be a steamboatman.

It was a dream he would carry for many years, but he was suddenly forced to put this and other boyhood dreams aside when his father died on March 24, 1847.

A few months earlier, the family had lost almost everything they owned when a land speculator failed to repay several thousand dollars John Clemens had loaned him. Clemens, desperately seeking some way to support his family, ran for election to the clerkship of Surrogate Court.

He was the favorite to win, but the appointment

was so vital to his family's economic survival, that he took no chances.

Judge Clemens, as he was called because he once served briefly as a justice of the peace, traveled on horseback from house to house in his effort to gain votes. Often he rode through rain and cold.

He won the election, but acquired a cough that grew steadily worse. He rode his horse to the swearing-in ceremonies in February, and was drenched by a rain and sleet storm on the way home. Within days, he was dead of pneumonia.

About the only property Sam's father had managed to hold onto was approximately 100,000 acres he had bought in Tennessee for less than a penny an acre.

He promised his family it would one day make them rich, and "went to his grave in the full belief that he had done us a kindness. It was a woeful mistake. . . . "

Sam was devastated by his father's death, not because he had ever been close to him, but because he felt guilty about not having been a better son. Throughout his childhood, he often felt guilt and remorse over things he had done, even if his motives were innocent.

When Sam cried and felt guilty on the day of his father's death, his mother told him: "It is all right, Sammy. What's done is done, and it does not matter to him any more; but here by the side of him now I want you to promise me — "

"I will promise anything," Sam said, crying, "if you don't make me go to school."

"No, Sammy," his mother replied, "you need not go to school any more. Only promise me to be a better boy. Promise not to break my heart."

Sam promised to be good, and his mother was satisfied. That night, and for several nights afterward, he walked in his sleep; then the sleepwalking stopped as suddenly as it had begun.

There was almost no money coming in for the Clemens family, but Sam stayed in school and worked at odd jobs for several months. Finally his mother was no longer able to feed or clothe him. She and Sam agreed that he should be apprenticed to Joseph Ament, owner of a print shop and a weekly Hannibal newspaper called the *Hannibal Courier*.

In many ways, the childhood of Samuel Langhorne Clemens was now over. He was about to take the first tentative steps on a road that would lead him not only to adulthood, but to fame and fortune even greater than his father's wildest dreams.

But first he would try to hold on to his childhood just a little longer.

2

OTHER WORLDS TO CONQUER

The apprentices in Ament's shop, like most apprentices throughout the United States at that time, received no money. Their pay was in food and clothing, plus the opportunity to learn a trade.

Sam was supposed to be given two new suits a year, "but one of the suits always failed to materialize and the other suit was not purchased so long as Mr. Ament's old clothes held out."

Ament also saved money by feeding his apprentices as little as possible.

Sam learned how to set type and sometimes acted as reporter or assistant editor. The majority of the material he set was poorly written, but sometimes he would be called on to set excerpts from the classics of the day.

This introduction to great literature awakened his interest in reading, and that interest became an obsession after he picked up a loose page on the street one afternoon on his way home from the printing shop.

The page was from a book about Joan of Arc, and it described her persecution by the English so well that Sam said he could feel her sufferings.

That stray page, he told a friend decades later, opened up to him the whole world of literature and awakened a passion for history that would last the rest of his life. He began to read everything he could get his hands on about Joan of Arc, the French wars, and history in general.

Though Sam had added the study of history to his busy schedule in the printing shop, he still found time to visit his family every day, keep in touch with his friends, and play the pranks he loved.

In 1851, Sam left to work for Orion, his oldest brother. Orion had returned home after living in St. Louis for several years while he learned the printing trade.

Twain's oldest brother, Orion, owner of the Hannibal Journal, *where Mark was employed as a typesetter.*

He was, said Twain, a dreamer who had "three hundred and sixty-five red-hot new eagernesses every year of his life . . . Every day he was the most joyous and hopeful man that ever was, I think, and also every day he was the most miserable man that ever was."

Orion borrowed $500 from an old farmer and bought a weekly newspaper called the *Hannibal Journal*. His brother Henry loved school and his mother had hoped he would become the family scholar, but Orion convinced her to let the twelve-year-old become one of his typesetters.

Sam also agreed to work for Orion when Ament refused to put him on the payroll. Orion promised Sam three dollars and a half a week, "which was an extravagant wage, but Orion was always generous, always liberal with everybody but himself. It cost him nothing in my case, for he never was able to pay me a single penny as long as I was with him."

Orion reduced the subscription price and advertising rates on the paper, thus ensuring that he would never be able to make a profit.

To make matters worse, most of the subscribers paid for their paper in cordwood, cabbages, and turnips, so the only cash Orion received came from advertisers.

Sam worked for his brother for three years, not only setting type, but also writing. Many of the stories he set were humorous sketches, and when Sam decided to try his hand at writing such sketches himself, Orion encouraged him. Sam also wrote satirical stories, local news reports, and poetry.

One week Orion made a trip to see if he could sell some of the Tennessee land his father had owned, and Sam took over as editor. It was an experience neither of them would ever forget.

First he wrote a story ridiculing a rival editor who had vowed to drown himself after being jilted by his girlfriend. Sam used the names of the people involved, and engraved an illustration showing the editor wading into the river with a stick to test the water's depth.

"Being satisfied with this effort I looked around for other worlds to conquer, and it struck me that it would make good, interesting matter to charge the editor of a neighboring country paper with a piece of gratuitous rascality and 'see him squirm.'"

Next Sam lampooned two prominent citizens, and topped off his efforts with disparaging remarks about a man who wrote poetry for the paper. The result was more than Sam had hoped for, and almost more than he could handle.

The country editor "pranced in next day with a warwhoop," the two prominent citizens threatened to sue for libel, the poet "departed for the South that night," and the jilted lover showed up at the office with a double-barreled shotgun, but when "he found that it was an infant (as he called me) that had done him the damage, he simply pulled my ears and went away."

Orion was not happy with Sam's actions, but "he softened when he looked at the accounts and saw that I had actually booked the unparalleled number of thirty-three new subscribers, and had the vegetables to show for it, cordwood, cabbage, beans, and unsalable turnips enough to run the family for two years!"

Sam's experience writing for the paper while Orion was away made him eager to see his work in print again, and he quickly wrote two humorous anecdotes and sent them off to the Philadelphia *Saturday Evening Post*. The *Post* didn't pay anything, but the editors accepted the stories.

"Seeing them in print was a joy which rather exceeded anything in that line I have ever experienced since," he said almost sixty years later.

The prosperity Sam had brought to the *Journal* proved to be temporary, and the paper continued its downhill slide. Sam, who was now eighteen, still had nothing to show for his years with Orion.

The end of his employment at the *Journal* came in the summer of 1853, when Orion refused to give him a few dollars to buy a secondhand gun. Apparently Sam wanted the gun simply because so many other men had them. He told his mother it was time for him to leave: He believed his brother hated him and that there was no longer a place for him in the home.

Mark Twain at the age of 18, the year he moved to New York.

Before he left, his mother made him hold one end of a New Testament while she held the other end.

"I want you to repeat after me, Sam, these words," she said. " 'I do solemnly swear that I will not throw a card or drink a drop of liquor while I am gone.' "

He repeated the oath, then kissed his mother.

"*Remember* that, Sam, and write to us," she told him.

He never lived in Hannibal again, but the fourteen years he had spent there would shape his life. The world would learn about Hannibal and his childhood from his books, and even when he was old, he would continue to seek inspiration from those far-off days.

When Sam left Hannibal, he took with him the

racism that had been bred into him by family, school, church, and state. As he grew older, he would spend much of his time trying to triumph over that bitter legacy, but for now he accepted it without question.

He traveled to St. Louis and found a job working in the composing room of the *Evening News* for several weeks, then he started out to see the world. In Sam's eyes the world was New York City.

Sam found work in New York at a printing shop that paid him four dollars a week " . . . and I found board in a sufficiently villainous mechanics'

A French woodcut of the interior of a print shop.

boarding-house in Duane Street.... My week's wage merely sufficed to pay board and lodging."

"You ask where I spend my evenings?" he wrote his sister Pamela. "Where do you suppose, with a free printer's library containing more than 4,000 volumes within a quarter of a mile of me, and nobody at home to talk to?"

He spent only four months in New York, then "went to Philadelphia and worked there some months as a 'sub' on the *Inquirer* and the *Public Ledger*. Finally I made a flying trip to Washington (D.C.) to see the sights there, and in 1854 I went back to the Mississippi Valley, sitting upright in the smoking-car two or three days and nights. When I reached St. Louis I was exhausted. I went to bed on board a steamboat that was bound for Muscatine."

The *Hannibal Journal* had failed not long after Sam left, and Orion bought another small weekly—the Muscatine, Iowa, *Journal*. He also married after falling in love with a young woman from Keokuk, Iowa, named Mollie.

Sam worked for Orion a few months, then moved to St. Louis. There he worked as a typesetter on the *Evening News*, before accepting Orion's offer of another job. The *Journal* had failed, but Orion purchased the Ben Franklin Book and Job Printing Office in Keokuk, and again lowered his prices so much he couldn't make any money.

While working in St. Louis, Sam's interest in read-

Twain's sister-in-law and brother, Mollie and Orion Clemens.

ing broadened when a young man he roomed with introduced him to the writings of Charles Dickens, Sir Walter Scott, and William Thackeray. When Sam moved to Keokuk, he often read late into the night, and carried a history book or a novel by Dickens as he walked the streets.

His world was also expanding in other ways at this time. It was at a printers' banquet in Keokuk that he made his first after-dinner speech. The audience loved his humor, and from then on the room was packed whenever he was scheduled to speak.

Sam enjoyed himself in Keokuk but, as usual, was paid nothing by Orion.

One snowy day the wind blew a piece of paper past him "and it lodged against a wall of a house. Something about the look of it attracted my attention and I gathered it in. It was a fifty-dollar bill, the only one I had ever seen, and the largest assemblage of money I had ever seen in one spot."

He advertised his find in the paper, but when no one had claimed it after four days, he bought a ticket for Cincinnati.

In Cincinnati, Sam found work in a printing office and settled into another boardinghouse. One of his fellow roomers was a man who owned a small library of books on philosophy, history, and science.

The man, a Scotchman named Macfarlane, introduced Sam for the first time to ideas about the nature of man that he had never heard before: "He said that man's heart was the only bad heart in the animal kingdom," that man was "the sole animal in whom was fully developed the base instinct called *patriotism*," and that "there was never a man who did not use his intellect daily all his life to advantage himself at other people's expense."

Sam was fascinated by these new ideas, and would develop many of them in his writings in the years to come.

One of the books he had read in Keokuk was about an exploration of the upper Amazon River. He was attracted by the explorer's discussion of coca and "made up my mind that I would go to the head-waters of the Amazon and collect coca and trade in it and make a fortune."

He promptly headed for New Orleans on the *Paul Jones*, an old steamboat piloted by Horace Bixby.

"When I got to New Orleans I inquired about ships leaving for Pará and discovered that there weren't any and learned that there probably wouldn't be any during that century," Sam said. "It had not occurred to me to inquire about these particulars before leaving Cincinnati, so there I was. I couldn't get to the Amazon. I had no friends in New Orleans and no money to speak of. I went to Horace Bixby and asked him to make a pilot out of me. He said he would do it for five hundred dollars, one hundred dollars cash in advance."

Sam helped steer the *Paul Jones* to St. Louis, where his sister Pamela lived, and borrowed the one hundred dollars from her husband, William Moffett.

"I entered upon the small enterprise of 'learning' twelve or thirteen hundred miles of the great Mississippi River with the easy confidence of my time of life," he wrote seventeen years later.

"If I had really known what I was about to require of my faculties, I should not have had the courage to begin."

But luckily for the eager twenty-one-year-old, and for generations of readers to come, he had no idea what was about to be required of his faculties.

Learning the river proved unbelievably hard for him at first, but in time he said it became "a wonderful book" delivering its most cherished secrets to him "as clearly as if it uttered them with a voice."

3

LEARNING THE GREAT RIVER

There were no reliable charts or other aids to navigation in 1857, and a cub pilot had to learn the river's shape and where the safe channels were. He had to remember the location of every sandbar, sunken wreck, and snag for over 1,000 miles. He had to be able to steer his boat in the daytime and in the nighttime, in clear weather and in weather so foggy he couldn't see the shorelines.

And he had to learn these things over and over, for the river was constantly changing. That was why each boat had a leadsman who sounded the water with a lead weight and then called out the depth: "Mark twain! [two fathoms, or twelve feet]. Mark three! [eighteen feet]. Quarter twain! [two and a quarter fathoms, or thirteen and a half feet]."

Sam's first attempt at piloting was not promising.

Bixby steered the *Paul Jones* close to several boats along the shore, then handed the wheel to him and said, "Here, take her; shave those steamships as close as you'd peel an apple."

Sam took the wheel, held his breath, and promptly headed the *Paul Jones* out toward the middle of the river.

"In half a minute I had a wide margin of safety intervening between the *Paul Jones* and the ships; and within ten seconds more I was set aside in disgrace, and Mr. Bixby was going into danger again and flaying me alive with abuse of my cowardice."

When Bixby had calmed down, he told Sam "the easy water" when they were going upriver was close

"The Mississippi in Time of Peace," lithograph by Currier and Ives, 1865, shows how the river would have looked when Twain was a pilot.

to shore, while the best place for the boat when they were coming downriver was out in the current.

"In my own mind," said Sam, "I resolved to be a down-river pilot and leave the up-streaming to people dead to prudence."

Bixby also kept calling out the names of places, such as: "This is Nine-Mile Point" or "This is Twelve-Mile Point."

Sam said all the places looked alike to him, and he wished Bixby would quit giving him so much useless information.

At last Bixby told Sam, "My boy, you must get a little memorandum book; and every time I tell you a thing, put it down right away. There's only one way to be a pilot, and that is to get this entire river by heart. You have to know it just like A B C."

So Sam bought a little book and began to keep notes. But every time he thought he was beginning to master the necessary knowledge, the captain or his chief would tell him countless other facts he needed to know.

"A clear starlight night throws such heavy shadows that, if you didn't know the shape of a shore perfectly, you would claw away from every bunch of timber, because you would take the black shadow of it for a solid cape," the chief told him.

". . . Then there's your pitch-dark night; the river is a very different shape on a pitch-dark night from what it is on a starlight night. . . . Then there's your gray mist. You take a night when there's one of these grisly, drizzly, gray mists, and then there isn't *any* particular shape to a shore . . . Well, then, different kinds of *moonlight* change the shape of the river in different ways."

Two things became "pretty apparent to me," Sam declared. "One was that in order to be a pilot a man had got to learn more than any one man ought to be allowed to know; and the other was that he must learn it all over again in a different way every twenty-four hours."

One day while Bixby was lecturing him on the importance of knowing the location and depth of several hundred places on the river, Sam said he was ready to quit because "I haven't got brains enough to be a pilot; and if I had I wouldn't have strength enough to carry them around, unless I went on crutches."

"Now drop that!" Bixby declared. "When I say I'll learn a man the river I mean it. And you can depend on it, I'll learn him or kill him."

So Sam kept learning. And when Bixby left the Mississippi several months later to pilot steamboats on the Missouri River, Sam continued to learn with other pilots.

In 1858, he served on the swift and popular *Pennsylvania*, a new steamer that carried passengers, mail, and merchandise. The pilothouse "was a sumptious glass temple; room enough to have a dance in," and "I began to take heart once more to believe that piloting was a romantic sort of occupation after all."

His good feelings were quickly dashed by the pilot, however. "He was a middle-aged, long, slim, bony, smooth-shaven, horse-faced, ignorant, stingy, malicious, snarling, fault-hunting mote-magnifying tyrant," Sam said of pilot William Brown.

Brown found fault with everything Sam did, and the resulting anger led Sam to lie awake nights imagining ways to kill his tormentor.

"I killed Brown every night for a month," he said, "not in old, stale, commonplace ways, but in new and picturesque ones — ways that were sometimes surprising for freshness of design and ghastly for situation and environment."

Sam had been on the river nearly a year now, but apprentice pilots received no wages, so Sam looked for a way to make money.

At the end of every voyage from St. Louis to New Orleans, the *Pennsylvania* waited a day or two before starting north again. Sam found work watching freight piles on the New Orleans levee from 7 P.M. to 7 A.M., and was paid three dollars a night.

"It was a desolate experience," he remembered, "watching there in the dark among those piles of freight; not a sound, not a living creature astir. But it was not a profitless one; I used to have inspirations as I sat there alone those nights. I used to imagine all sorts of situations and possibilities. Those things got into my books by and by and furnished me with many a chapter. I can trace the effect of those nights through most of my books in one way and another."

Sam's brother Henry was working as a clerk on the *Pennsylvania*. The two of them stayed with Pamela and their brother-in-law when the boat was docked in St. Louis, and Henry left the house late every night to start his duties on the ship.

One night Sam dreamed that Henry had died.

"In the morning, when I awoke, I had been dreaming, and the dream was so vivid, so like reality, that it deceived me and I thought it *was* real. In the dream I had seen Henry a corpse. He lay in a metallic burial case. He was dressed in a suit of my clothing and on his breast lay a great bouquet of flowers, mainly white roses, with a red rose in the center."

Sam told Pamela about the dream, and then put it out of his mind. Not long afterward, the brothers left on another trip to New Orleans on the *Pennsylvania*.

When the *Pennsylvania* reached New Orleans, Sam left the boat and joined the Memphis-bound *A.T. Lacy*, while Henry remained on the *Pennsylvania*.

Two days later the *Pennsylvania* left New Orleans for St. Louis, followed in another two days by the *Lacy*.

"We touched at Greenville, Mississippi, a couple of days out," Sam said, "and somebody shouted: 'The

Pennsylvania is blown up at Ship Island, and a hundred and fifty lives lost!' "

Four of the *Pennsylvania*'s eight boilers had exploded, sending the front third of the ship into the sky. Then it came down onto the cabins and the three or four hundred deck passengers, "a mountain of riddled and chaotic rubbish — and then, after a little, fire broke out."

A cloud of scalding steam killed all who breathed it. Many people were crippled by the blast, while others burned to death trapped in the rubble. The explosion drove an iron crowbar through one man's chest.

Henry was blown into the water and started swimming toward shore, but though he had been fatally scalded, he thought he wasn't hurt and swam back to the boat.

Sam found him on a mattress "on the floor of a great hall" in Memphis, one among more than forty forms in two long rows, "and every face and head a shapeless wad of loose raw cotton. It was a gruesome spectacle."

Sam sat by his brother's bedside day and night, and prayed desperately for his survival, but it was no use.

"Long before this reaches you, my poor Henry — my darling, my pride, my glory, my all, will have finished his blameless career, and the light of my life will have gone out in utter darkness," Sam wrote Orion's wife, Mollie.

Twain's younger brother Henry, who was fatally scalded at the age of 20 aboard the Pennsylvania.

"O, God! this is hard to bear. Hardened, hopeless — aye, lost — lost and ruined sinner as I am — I, even I, have humbled myself to the ground and prayed as never a man prayed before, that the Great God might let this cup pass from me — that he would strike me to earth, but spare my brother. . . . "

But on the evening of the sixth day, Henry's "wandering mind busied itself with matters far away, and his nerveless fingers 'picked at his coverlet.' His hour had struck; we bore him to the death-room, poor boy."

Henry was twenty years old; Sam was twenty-two.

Almost all the victims were buried in coffins of unpainted white pine, but while Sam was sleeping in a nearby house, "some of the ladies of Memphis had made up a fund of sixty dollars and bought a metallic case, and when I came back and entered the dead-room Henry lay in that open case and he was dressed in a suit of my clothing. I recognized instantly that my dream of several weeks before was here exactly reproduced, so far as these details went — and I think I missed one detail, but that one was immediately supplied, for just then an elderly lady entered the place with a large bouquet consisting mainly of white roses, and in the center of it was a red rose and she laid it on his breast."

Henry — wanting to be like his older brother — had followed him onto the river, and Sam always blamed himself for his brother's death. He reasoned that if he hadn't signed on as a cub pilot, Henry would not have ended up on the *Pennsylvania* and would still be alive.

Grief and guilt threatened to consume him, and he seemed to be losing his mind. Friends asked a man to escort Sam to St. Louis, where his mother tried to comfort him. Gradually the pall that had fallen over his life began to lift, and he returned to the river.

On April 9, 1859, he received his Pilot's Certificate from the inspectors for the District of St. Louis. He

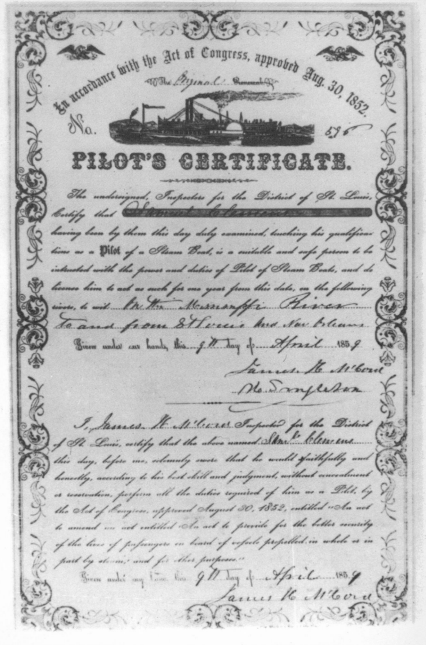

Mark Twain's pilot's certificate, issued in 1859.

"had mastered the language of this water, and had come to know every trifling feature that bordered the great river as familiarly as I knew the letters of the alphabet . . ."

But Sam realized that in learning the river so thoroughly he had also "lost something which could never be restored to me while I lived. All the grace, the beauty, the poetry, had gone out of the majestic river! . . ."

Sam's career as a pilot, which he once thought would last the rest of his life, came to an abrupt end with the outbreak of the Civil War in 1861. Both the Union and the Confederacy warned that pilots might be shot, and President Abraham Lincoln said the Union was considering drafting pilots who stayed on the river.

One of Sam's nieces said he "was obsessed with the fear that he might be arrested by government agents and forced to act as pilot on a government gunboat while a man stood by with a pistol ready to shoot him if he showed the least sign of a false move."

He returned to visit Hannibal as a passenger on the last steamer to make the trip from New Orleans to St. Louis.

In Hannibal, as elsewhere throughout the United States, neighbors and families had split over whether to support the Union or the Confederacy. In the 1860 presidential election, Orion — who had sometimes used the *Hannibal Journal* to fight for the rights of free black residents — voted for Lincoln.

Sam voted for the Constitutional Union Party, a coalition that supported slavery and recent U.S. Supreme Court decisions that protected slavery. In years to come he would bitterly denounce all forms of slavery and oppression, but in the summer of 1861, he decided to join a group of friends to fight for the Confederacy. They were all from Marion County, and they called themselves the Marion Rangers.

The group of boyhood friends elected each other to various officers' ranks, with Sam being made a second lieutenant. By the time they finished appointing officers, there were only three privates left.

Most of Missouri was already in Union hands, so the company drilled secretly near Hannibal for a while, then retreated to a safer area. There they were officially sworn in by a Colonel Ralls, who talked his neighbors into contributing to the group.

Among the contributions were several cast-off horses and mules, so the infantry company suddenly became a cavalry company. Sam was given Paint Brush, a small yellow mule with a tail trimmed so it looked like a brush.

One day some farmers brought word that a detachment of Union soldiers was in the area, with orders to hang any members of outfits like Sam's.

The company's captain, Tom Lyman, wanted to stay where they were, but everyone else voted to retreat. Their only question was which direction to head in.

The company hid at a nearby farmhouse for several days, sleeping in a corncrib. Finally they ventured forth again. One day, almost out of food, they headed for the farm of a friend named Colonel Bill Splawn.

It was dark when they arrived, so rather than wake Splawn and his family, the Rangers crept into a hayloft to sleep. In a few moments, someone yelled, "Fire!"

A careless smoker had set the hay on fire, and Sam awoke to find the blaze almost under him. In a frantic effort to escape, he rolled out of a window-size opening into the barnyard several feet below.

Sam sprained one ankle in the fall, but forgot his pain when the other Rangers tossed burning hay on top of him. Their laughter after the incident did nothing to soothe his anger.

The next morning they set out again, but got no farther than the next farm. Sam's ankle had swollen so badly he was put to bed, where he stayed several weeks.

His career as a soldier was over.

"I could have become a [good] soldier myself, if I

had waited," he said. "I had got part of it learned, I knew more about retreating than the man that invented retreating."

Sam visited with Orion, who was broke as usual. But Orion's luck had suddenly changed. Edward Bates, a friend who was attorney general in President Lincoln's cabinet, had recently managed to have him appointed secretary of the newly created Territory of Nevada. All Orion needed was the money to get there.

He asked his brother to go with him, both to supply the money and "to wean Sam away from his rebel cause."

Sam agreed, and Orion appointed him private secretary to the secretary, a job that paid no money.

On July 26, 1861, they "cleared for that country in the overland stagecoach, I paying the fares, which were pretty heavy . . . "

As the coach began the twenty-day journey from St. Joseph, Missouri, to Carson City, Nevada, Sam said he felt "an exhilarating sense of emancipation from all sorts of cares and responsibilities, that almost made us feel that the years we had spent in the close, hot city, toiling and slaving, had been wasted and thrown away. We were spinning along through Kansas, and in the course of an hour and a half we were fairly abroad on the great Plains."

He only planned to stay in Nevada three months.

But instead of three months, it would be six "uncommonly long years" before he returned east. And when he came back, it would not be as Samuel Clemens, riverboat pilot, but as Mark Twain: a man with "some reputation in the Atlantic states."

4

MY NAME IS CLEMENS

It was a hot, dusty day when Sam and Orion arrived in Carson City, the capital of Nevada Territory. There were only 2,000 residents in the town where "a soaring dust-drift about the size of the United States set up edge-wise, came every afternoon."

The wind was called the Washoe Zephyr ("Washoe" was a nickname for Nevada), and Sam said it covered him so completely with alkali dust "you'd thought I worked in a starch factory and boarded in a flour barrel."

The main street "consisted of four or five blocks of little white frame stores . . . packed close together, side by side, as if room were scarce in that mighty plain. The sidewalk was of boards that were more or less loose and inclined to rattle when walked upon. In the middle of the town, opposite the stores, was the 'plaza' which is native to all towns beyond the Rocky Mountains — a large, unfenced, level vacancy. . . . Two other sides of the plaza were faced by stores, offices and stables."

The town was nestled on the edge of a vast desert, "walled in by barren, snow-clad mountains. There was not a tree in sight. There was no vegetation but the endless sage-brush and grease-wood. All nature was gray with it."

Soon after Sam and Orion stepped down from the stagecoach, a man on horseback introduced himself as Mr. Harris. He began to talk to them, then suddenly stopped.

"I'll have to get you to excuse me a minute," he declared, "yonder is the witness that swore I helped to rob the California coach — a piece of impertinent intermeddling, sir, for I am not even acquainted with the man."

Harris rode over to the stranger, who was mending a whiplash. They argued fiercely, then emptied their six-shooters at each other.

After they ran out of ammunition, "Mr. Harris rode by with a polite nod, homeward bound, with a bullet through one of his lungs, and several in his hips; and from them issued little rivulets of blood that coursed down the horse's sides and made the animal look quite picturesque. I never saw Harris shoot a man after that but it recalled to mind that first day in Carson."

Within two or three weeks, Sam was walking around like an old-time resident, complete with slouched hat, wool shirt, and pants shoved into the tops of his boots.

He was fascinated with the wild, exciting life

around him and quickly made up his mind to stay more than three months. Not long afterward, Sam completed his transformation into his version of a western frontiersman by growing a mustache and beard, and arming himself with an old navy revolver.

"I felt rowdyish and bully," he said. "It seemed to me that nothing could be so fine and so romantic."

There was little for him to do as Orion's secretary, so he concentrated on having fun and becoming a "real" westerner.

Every day in Carson City, he saw magnificent horsemanship, and so he decided to buy a horse for twenty-seven dollars.

The first time Sam tried to ride him, "he placed all his feet in a bunch together, lowered his back, and then suddenly arched it upward, and shot me straight into the air a matter of three or four feet! I came as straight down again, lit in the saddle, went instantly up again, came down almost on the high pommel, shot up again, and came down on the horse's neck — all in the space of three or four seconds. . . . The third time I went up I heard a stranger say: 'Oh, *don't* he buck, though!'"

Sam soon tried to give the horse away, but no one would take him: "Parties said earthquakes were handy enough on the Pacific coast — they did not wish to own one."

During his first few weeks in the territory, Sam also found time to anger people with his pro-Southern, anti-Union talk.

Not long before he and Orion arrived in Nevada, the territory's voters had overwhemingly rejected a proposal to become a state. Many voters opposed the proposal because it would have permitted free black people to live in Nevada.

Nevada territorial law in 1861 made it a crime punishable by fine, imprisonment, or being sold into slavery, for a free black person to try and settle permanently in Nevada. Many other areas of the United States had similar laws, especially in the South, Midwest, and West.

But although there was strong anti-black, pro-South sentiment in Nevada, Sam managed to enrage several people with the vehemence of his defense of the South. He even kept a scrapbook of newspaper articles praising secessionist sentiment in the West.

He loved to hang out in saloons, and at some point apparently bragged that he had been a first lieutenant in the regular Confederate Army.

Governor James Nye, Orion's boss, called Sam a "damned secessionist," and a judge in Virginia City threatened to whip him "on sight." Even Southern sympathizers were angered when they found out Sam had been just a second lieutenant in a ragtag group that spent most of its time retreating.

All of this was embarrassing to Orion, who served

An engraving of traffic in the treacherous Sierra Nevada mountains.

as acting governor when Nye was in Washington, and he was glad when Sam decided to explore the surrounding countryside.

Many people were trying to get rich by staking timber claims in the area around Lake Bigler (now called Lake Tahoe), so Sam and a friend named John Kinney decided to do the same. Friends offered the use of their cabin, rations, and tools.

The two decided to walk the eleven miles from Carson City to the lake, each carrying an axe and two blankets. They apparently didn't know they would run into deep valleys and high mountains.

There were vast stretches of timber around the lake, and the next day Sam and John claimed three hundred acres of it by sticking notices on a tree. In order to make their claim legal, the two had to fence it in and build a house. The fence consisted of six trees they cut down, which they found "such heartbreaking work that we decided to 'rest our case' on those; if they held the property, well and good; if they didn't, let the property spill out through the gaps. . . . "

They started to build a log house, but changed their minds after cutting and trimming one log. Then they decided to build the house out of saplings, but after cutting and trimming two saplings, they decided "a still modester architecture would satisfy the law." Finally they settled on building a "brush" house, which had "a strong family resemblance to the surrounding vegetation. But we were satisfied with it."

The next few days were as happy as any Sam had known. But the idyllic experience came to an abrupt end one evening when he lit the cooking fire, then went off to get the frying pan.

"While I was at this, I heard a shout from Johnny, and looking up I saw that my fire was galloping all over the premises!"

Dry pine needles that carpeted the floor were "touched off as if they were gunpowder. It was wonderful to see with what fierce speed the tall sheet of flame travelled."

Sam and John hid in the boat while the fire roared

along the shore, then exploded into canyons and up surrounding hills, before finally passing out of sight several hours later.

They spent the night ashore, then took the boat out again the next day. They had not gone far, however, when a storm came up.

The storm grew worse, "and it became evident that it was better to take the hazard of beaching the boat than go down in a hundred fathoms of water; so we ran in. . . . The instant the bow struck, a wave came over the stern that washed crew and cargo ashore, and saved a deal of trouble."

That was the end of Sam's attempts to become a timber magnate, but he quickly looked for other ways to get rich quick, as everyone around him seemed to be doing.

Each day on the streets of Carson City, he saw prospecting parties leaving for the mountains to search for silver. In the saloons, he heard tales of men and women grown rich overnight, and in each edition of the newspapers he read about the latest discovery of a rich vein of silver at some new mine: the "Ophir," the "Golden Fleece," the "Bald Eagle and Mary Ann," the "Last Chance," the "Esmeralda."

"I would have been more or less than human if I had not gone mad like the rest," he said. "Cart-loads of solid silver bricks . . . were arriving from the mills every day, and such sights as that gave substance to the wild talk about me. I succumbed and grew as frenzied as the rest."

In December 1861, Sam and three other men — two young lawyers and a sixty-year-old blacksmith named Tillou — pushed two old horses and the wagonload of provisions and mining tools the horses were supposed to be hauling, through 200 miles of sand and snow.

Along the way they passed new graves and the charred ruins of shacks burned during a recent war between whites and Paiute warriors. Discovery of gold and silver in Nevada, as elsewhere in the West,

Members of the Paiute tribe, who were forced to defend their land from prospectors.

often led to bloodshed when prospectors invaded Native American lands.

The weary journey ended on the fifteenth day, when the four arrived at Unionville, Humboldt County, in a driving snowstorm. Unionville consisted of six cabins along one side of a deep canyon and five cabins facing them, with high mountain walls rising from both sides of the canyon.

The four men built a small cabin with a canvas roof, leaving one corner open to act as a chimney.

Sam, who was disappointed at not finding silver lying all around and glittering in the sun, decided he was prepared to spend as much as two weeks finding enough silver to make him rich.

And so they began their search for wealth, laboriously digging in the mountainside with picks and shovels, then blasting with dynamite when they could go no further. They called their first mine "Monarch of the Mountains."

Shares or "feet" in mines could be purchased for very little money down, and in a short while Sam and his friends owned parts of several other mines.

Sam vowed not to return east until he was rich, which he was certain would be soon, but in the meantime there was barely enough money to buy food.

"Stint yourself as much as possible," he wrote Orion, who was financing the prospecting venture, "and lay up $100 or $150, subject to my call . . ."

Sam promised Orion they would be wealthy capitalists within two years, but the cost of food and tools was prohibitive, and Sam and the others spent Orion's money as fast as he sent it.

They started out each morning with high hopes, but ended up each night with nothing but more worthless rocks to show for their labor.

In April 1862, he and several friends tried their luck in Aurora, a booming mining town in the Sierra Nevada Mountains near the California border. Sam had been there briefly the previous fall, but hadn't had time to do any mining.

Snow was several feet deep, and the men spent much of their time planning the tunnels they would

One of the first underground mining photos, taken in 1868 of Savage Mine, Comstock Lode, Virginia City, Nevada.

dig when the weather improved, or estimating the wealth the mines would bring them.

Sometimes Sam felt the need to be alone, and would go for solitary walks far from camp.

Often during the long, bleak evenings, he entertained his companions with tall tales, but at other times he sat as if lost in his own thoughts.

"He was the life of the camp," one friend remembered, "but sometimes there would come a reaction and he would hardly speak for a day or two."

He also wrote letters to the Virginia City *Territorial Enterprise*, experimenting with different styles of writing in his accounts of Nevada life.

The most popular of the letters, which he signed with the pen name "Josh," were those that were humorous.

Sam asked Orion to put all his *Enterprise* letters into a scrapbook, in case he needed the originals.

"Those Enterprise fellows make perfect nonsense of my letters, like all d — d fool printers, they can't follow the punctuation as it is in the manuscript," he wrote his brother. "They have . . . made a mass of senseless, d — d stupidity out of my last letter."

Having to stay in one place very long was something Sam hated, as he made very plain in a letter to Orion: "I have now been here over two months," he wrote, "and have accomplished a great deal — but I know, and you know, that I cannot double that time in any one place without a miracle. I have been here as long, now, as it is in my nature to stay in one place — and from this out I shall feel as much like a prisoner as if I were in the county jail."

But he was determined to stick it out awhile longer, even though he was beginning to feel disappointment after so many failures. The money he had saved from his wages as a pilot was long gone, and the cost of food was astronomical. Flour cost $100 a barrel when he first arrived in Aurora, and rarely dipped below $40 a barrel.

"I owe about 45 or $50, and have got about $45 in my pocket," he wrote Orion. "But how in the h — l I am going to live on something over $100 until October or November, is singular. The fact is, I must have something to do; and that *shortly*, too."

He begged Orion to use his influence to try and get him work as a correspondent for the *Sacramento Union*, the Carson City *Silver Age*, or on a newspaper the chief clerk of the territorial legislature was talking about starting.

Two years earlier, two young printers from San Francisco bought the *Territorial Enterprise*, a weekly paper that was on the verge of collapse, and turned it into a huge success by keeping "the universe thoroughly posted concerning murders and street fights . . . and the thousand other things which it is in the province of local reporters to keep track of and magnify into undue importance for the instruction of the readers of a great daily newspaper."

The two young printers were Denis McCarthy and Joseph Goodman. William Barstow was the business manager of the paper.

"That is the sort of thing we want," Goodman said of Sam's humorous letters. "Write to him, Barstow, and ask him if he wants to come up here."

Barstow wrote, offering the job of city editor at $25 a week. But Sam hesitated "when I thought of my inexperience and consequent unfitness for the position — and straightway, on top of this, my long array of failures rose up before me. Yet if I refused this place I must presently become dependent upon somebody for my bread. . . . So I was scared into being a city editor."

Sam also hesitated because he still hoped to be hired by another paper as its California correspondent, but when no other offer came, he reluctantly headed to Virginia City.

It was 130 miles to the northeast and Sam walked all the way, arriving at the *Enterprise* office on a hot day in late September 1862.

When he walked into the office, wrote a friend several decades later, it was as "the master of the world's widest estate come to claim his kingdom."

But he hardly looked the part, and almost certainly didn't feel it. He wore a battered hat, was covered with alkali dust, and had a beard that hung halfway to his waist.

Sam dropped a blanket roll from his shoulders and slipped wearily into a chair.

When McCarthy asked what he wanted, he replied: "My name is Clemens, and I've come to write for the paper."

5

MARK TWAIN — A PLEASANT SOUND

The *Enterprise* was Nevada's oldest newspaper and the largest daily between San Francisco and Chicago. The offices were on North C Street, in the heart of the biggest and richest mining camp in the West.

Virginia City sat halfway up 7,200-foot Mt. Davidson, atop the fabulously rich Comstock Lode. The lode, named after the man who discovered it (Henry "Old Pancake" Comstock), was the world's wealthiest known silver deposit.

Though the deposit was discovered in 1857, the public didn't learn about it until 1859. Now men, some with women and children, flocked to Virginia City from all over the world to seek their fortunes.

The plank sidewalks swarmed with miners, mine owners, prospectors, traders, and adventurers of every kind. Most men carried guns, including the five editors and twenty-three printers at the *Enterprise*.

When a stranger arrived in a new mining district, Sam said, "they did not inquire if he was capable, honest, industrious, but — had he killed his man? . . . The deference that was paid to a desper-

An American engraving, 1878, of the main street of Virginia City, Nevada.

ado of wide reputation and who 'kept his private graveyard,' as the phrase went, was marked, and cheerfully accorded."

Virginia City's streets were so jammed with wagons, carts, and stagecoaches that people trying to cross C Street in buggies often had to wait half an hour.

The Comstock Lode ran straight through town, and blasting, picking, and shoveling went on twenty-four hours a day in the mines beneath the town. Thunderous blasts deep in the earth often rattled the newspaper's windows and shook the chairs.

Sam was fascinated by the excitement of Virginia City, but uncertain about how to do his job.

Goodman told him to "go all over town and ask all sorts of people all sorts of questions, make notes of the information gained, and write them out for publication."

Going all over town wasn't as easy as it sounded, for Mt. Davidson was so steep that "the entire town had a slant to it like a roof. Each street was a terrace, and from each to the next street below the descent was forty or fifty feet. . . . It was a laborious climb, in that thin atmosphere, to ascend from D to A street, and you were panting and out of breath when you got there. . . . "

Throughout his career as a reporter, Sam would often show a remarkable indifference to the facts. If the facts sounded better mixed in with fiction, then Sam threw in the fiction.

When he read his mixtures of fact and fiction in the columns of the *Enterprise*, Sam said, "I felt that I had found my legitimate occupation at last."

He quickly settled into a comfortable routine at the paper, and was soon adding commentary, humorous exaggerations, and hoaxes to his everyday reporting.

In November, Goodman sent him down to Carson City to cover the territorial legislature, which was in session sixty days a year. Governor Nye was gone most of the time, so Orion was acting governor. Sam was quickly accepted by the politicians, even though many of his articles were harshly critical of them.

He wrote a daily report on legislative business and an article every Saturday about different personalities (all of his writings were in the form of letters). Later he would say that his experiences with two sessions of the legislature, and one session covering the U.S. Congress, allowed him "to know personally three sample bodies of the smallest minds and the selfishest souls and the cowardliest hearts that God makes."

On a brief trip to Virginia City, he told Goodman he wanted to start signing his articles, which were being reprinted in papers all along the West Coast.

The editor asked if he wanted to use "Josh," and Sam replied:

"No, I want to sign them 'Mark Twain.' It is an old river term, a leads-man's call, signifying two fathoms — twelve feet. It has a richness about it; it was always a pleasant sound for a pilot to hear on a dark night; it means safe water."

Many writers used pen names at the time, especially writers of humor. The first article bearing the signature of "Mark Twain" appeared in the *Enterprise* on February 3, 1863, and was called "The Unreliable."

"The Unreliable" was a reporter named Clement Rice, who covered the legislature for the Virginia City *Daily Union*. It was common practice for reporters on rival papers in Virginia City to ridicule each other in print, and "Mark" said that Rice had attended a local convention only "for the purpose of distorting the facts."

"The Unreliable" became more and more prominent in the weekly articles, which now all bore the signature of "Mark Twain." Soon politicians, readers, and most of Sam's friends were calling him "Mark."

"The papers of the Coast took it up," wrote his friend and biographer, Albert Bigelow Paine, "and within a period to be measured by weeks he was no longer 'Sam' or 'Clemens' or 'that bright chap on the *Enterprise*,' but 'Mark' — 'Mark Twain.' No *nom de plume* was ever so quickly and generally accepted as that."

"Everybody knows me," he proudly wrote his mother, "& I fare like a prince wherever I go, be it on this side of the mountains or the other. And I am proud to say I am the most conceited ass in the Territory."

His writing hadn't changed, but people could now attach a personality to the articles. Politicians were so eager to curry his favor, they defeated laws he wanted defeated and passed laws he wanted passed.

"I was a mighty heavy wire-puller at the last Legislature," he told his mother. "I passed every bill I worked for, & on a bet, I killed a bill by a three-fourths vote in the House after it had passed the Council unanimously."

He even persuaded the legislators to pass a law that brought unaccustomed prosperity to Orion. The law required every corporation doing business in the territory to have its charter recorded by Orion, who collected a fee for each transaction. As a result, Twain's perennially poor brother was soon receiving an average of $1,000 a month in gold for his recording services (paper money had not been introduced in Nevada at this time).

A lithograph of Virginia City, Nevada, in 1861.

When Twain returned to Virginia City at the end of the session, it was as a man famous throughout the territory. His salary was doubled, but he rarely needed to spend it and sometimes forgot to collect it. People were always giving him and the other reporters free "feet" in their mines.

Miners did this so the reporters would write favorably about their mines, and thus raise the price of the stock, and many other people routinely gave the reporters mining feet as a gesture of friendship.

"Many a time friends gave us as much as twenty-five feet of stock that was selling at twenty-five dollars a foot," Twain said, "and they thought no more of it than they would of offering a guest a cigar. These were 'flush times' indeed! I thought they were going to last always, but somehow I never was much of a prophet."

In December 1863, the humorist Artemus Ward arrived in Virginia City on a nationwide lecture tour. Ward, whose real name was Charles Browne, was so popular President Lincoln often interrupted cabinet meetings to read his stories aloud.

Twain and Ward hit it off immediately, and spent the next several days roaming the town at all hours of the day and night. Ward advised Twain to move to New York City, where his name would become much more widely known, but Twain decided to remain in Nevada even though he was increasingly restless.

Ward's praise of his humor-writing talent and his

Humorist Artemus Ward (1834–1867), who befriended Twain in Virginia City, Nevada, in 1863.

advice to Twain to "leave sage-brush obscurity," had their effect, however. Not long afterward, Mark Twain wrote an article for a literary publication called the New York *Sunday Mercury*.

"I cannot write regularly for the *Mercury*, of course, I sha'n't have time," he said in a letter to his mother. "But sometimes I throw off a pearl before these swine here (there's no self-conceit about that, I beg you to observe) which ought, for the eternal welfare of my race to have a more extensive circulation than is offered by a local daily paper."

Almost immediately after Ward left town, Twain went back to Carson City to cover the legislature. While in Carson City, he stayed with Orion, his wife,

Mollie, and the couple's eight-year-old daughter Jennie.

Living with Orion's family was a welcome change from the bachelor life he'd known almost continuously since leaving Hannibal over a decade before, but this pleasant interlude suddenly came to a tragic end.

An epidemic was sweeping the area. The doctors called the sickness "spotted fever," but it was probably cerebrospinal meningitis. Jennie became sick on a Sunday morning and died four days later. The legislature adjourned to attend her funeral.

The brokenhearted Twain followed the coffin to the cemetery, just as he had followed the coffins of his brother Benjamin, who died when Mark was seven years old, his father, and his beloved Henry.

Two days after the funeral, he bitterly attacked the local undertaker, who owned the only respectable cemetery in town. He was, said Twain in an article in the *Enterprise*, a man who "charges a hundred and fifty dollars for a pine coffin that cost him twenty or thirty, and fifty dollars for a grave that did not cost him ten — and this at a time when his ghastly services are required at least seven times a week."

Mark Twain tried, as he would often try in the future, to deal with his grief and anger by channeling them into writing.

Shortly after Jennie's death, Goodman left for a vacation and Twain had to take over as chief editor.

Within a few days he had antagonized so many people with his editorials that four of them threatened to
horsewhip him and two challenged him to a duel.

In the most serious incident, Twain accused some
of Carson City's leading women of sending money to
a miscegenation society to promote sexual relations
between blacks and whites. The charge was probably the most volatile that could be made in the racial
climate of the time.

A rival editor printed a letter attacking Twain, and
several of the ladies' husbands talked of challenging
him to a duel. Twain quickly borrowed money from
Orion and left town.

Many people were glad to see him go, but a reporter for the *Daily Old Piute* expressed a more
widespread opinion when he wrote: "The world
is blank . . . and we are childless. We shall miss
Mark . . . to know him was to love him . . . God bless
you, Mark! be virtuous and happy."

6

BEST-KNOWN HONEST MAN ON THE COAST

Mark Twain arrived in San Francisco at the end of May 1864, and soon found a job working as the only reporter on the *Morning Call*. He still dreamed of becoming rich from his mining stocks, and had carried them with him in his trunk. In the meantime, however, he needed money to live on.

Working for the *Call* turned out to be a dreary experience. He had to follow a strict schedule that began with a visit to the police court at nine in the morning, and ended with a late-night round of six theaters.

There was little opportunity for the kind of colorful and creative writing he did at the *Enterprise*. Twain became especially angry when the paper refused to print his attacks on corrupt politicians and policemen. He was also becoming increasingly aware of injustices against the powerless, though he still clung to most of his racism.

One day he wrote about some butchers "who set their dogs on a Chinaman who was quietly passing with a basket of clothes on his head; and while the dogs mutilated his flesh, a butcher increased the hi-

Miners, 1852, including immigrant Chinese, whom Twain felt were victims of prejudice.

larity of the occasion by knocking some of the Chinaman's teeth down his throat with half a brick."

It was the kind of experience that occurred almost daily, while the police stood by and watched, or joined in the brutality.

Twain hurried to the newspaper and wrote a fiery article denouncing the incident, but the editor refused to print it.

When Twain asked why, he was told that the *Call* "gathered its livelihood from the poor and must respect their prejudices or perish."

The refusal to print his article snuffed out the little interest Twain had in his work at the *Call*, and he even considered accepting a job as a government pilot on the Mississippi, for a salary of $300 a month.

But he continued to write, and briefly contributed articles to *The Golden Era*, California's first literary publication. The *Era* wasn't "high-toned" enough for him, however, and he began to write for a new literary weekly, *The Californian*.

In a letter to his mother, Twain bragged that *The Californian* "circulates among the highest class of the community, & is the best weekly literary paper in the United States . . . "

His employment at the *Call* came to an abrupt end after four months, when he resigned with the wholehearted approval of the owner.

For the next few weeks, Twain existed on the money he received from *The Californian*, which was only about $12 an article.

He still had his mining stocks, but most of them were now worth little or nothing, because production was steadily declining in the mines. He managed to scrape up $300, probably by selling the last few valuable stocks, and left San Francisco for a remote cabin in the Sierra Nevada Mountains about 100 miles to the east, at a place called Jackass Hill.

Twain probably hoped to find gold during his visit to the mountains, and spent a few days searching for it. But gradually he realized that gold was being handed to him in another form — the stories told by the miners.

And so he began to concentrate less on the "pocket mining" they were doing (using shovels to search for gold in pockets just below the surface), and more on listening to the miners' anecdotes and tall tales.

In late January he went to Angels Camp, a nearby mining town. Most of his time was spent sitting around talking, with the men repeating stories they'd told each other for years.

One of the best storytellers was Ben Coon, an ex-miner who was proprietor of a hotel. Coon's favorite story was about a jumping frog. It was an old story that had been told in mining camps for years, but Twain was fascinated by it.

The notebook he was keeping at this time had a lot of jottings in it, including entries like "Rained all day," and "Same old diet."

But on one page he wrote: "Coleman with his jumping frog — bet a stranger $50. — stranger had no frog and C. got him one: — In the meantime stranger filled C's frog full of shot and he couldn't jump. The Stranger's frog won."

When Twain returned to Jackass Hill, he began work on the Jumping Frog story. He used to say: "If I can write that story the way Ben Coon told it, that frog will jump around the world."

Near the end of February, Twain returned to San

Francisco, and was again faced with the problem of paying rent and buying food.

He made a precarious living writing articles for *The Californian* and two or three other publications, using some of the material he'd gathered in the mountains. The Civil War ended a month after his return to the city, but he didn't even bother to mention this in his writings.

After a few weeks, Joe Goodman came to his financial rescue by hiring him as the *Enterprise*'s San Francisco correspondent at $100 a month.

Once again Twain was free to write the scathing articles he loved so well, and he wasted no time getting started. In a series of articles denouncing the police, he described the brutality he saw them commit on a routine basis.

Many newspaper editors were so offended by his critical comments about society — including attacks on clergymen he accused of putting money ahead of religious beliefs — that they stopped reprinting his writings.

Whereas Mark Twain had previously been called the Wild Humorist of the Sage Brush Hills, now he was even more widely known as the Moralist of the Main.

He spent the next few months writing for newspaper and literary periodicals, and his humorous articles were the most widely reprinted. In September 1865, the New York *Round Table* predicted that

A cartoon of Twain riding The Celebrated Jumping Frog of Caleveras County.

the "merry gentleman . . . who signs himself 'Mark Twain' . . . may one day take rank among the brightest of our wits."

Twain had apparently doubted his abilities as a humorous writer until he started hearing such praises. He also seemed to feel that humorous writing was an inferior kind of writing.

In a letter to Orion the day after he completed "Jim Smiley and His Jumping Frog," a sketch based on Coon's story, he said: "I never had but two *powerful* ambitions in my life. One was to be a pilot, & the other a preacher of the gospel. I accomplished the one & failed in the other, *because* I could not supply myself with the necessary stock in trade — i.e., religion. . . . But I *have* had a 'call' to literature, of a low order — i.e., humorous. It is nothing to be proud of, but it is my strongest suit. . . . "

He said that he should long ago have given up meddling with "things for which I was by nature unfitted & turned my attention to seriously scribbling to excite the *laughter* of God's creatures. Poor, pitiful business!"

The letter contained three themes that would haunt him the rest of his life: the fact that the fame he might achieve would come to him through humorous writing, "unworthy & evanescent though it must of necessity be," his inability to find comfort in traditional religious beliefs, and his deep-rooted fear of financial ruin.

The next month the New York *Saturday Press* printed "Jim Smiley and His Jumping Frog," the story that would make Twain famous and later be retitled "The Celebrated Jumping Frog of Calaveras County."

He had sent it to a New York publisher at the suggestion of Artemus Ward. But the publisher, a man named Carleton, didn't think much of the story and sent it on to the editor of the *Saturday Press*, a dying periodical that was about to print its last issue.

The story was an immediate hit and, while the frog didn't jump all over the world, it jumped onto newspapers throughout the United States and England.

The New York correspondent for the San Francisco *Alta* said the story "has set all New York in a roar, and he may be said to have made his mark." James Russell Lowell, distinguished poet, essayist, and critic, said the "Jumping Frog" was the finest piece of humorous writing ever produced in the United States.

"Mark Twain" was now on the lips of many people who had never heard of him before, though Mark insisted that "it was only the frog that was celebrated. It wasn't I. I was still an obscurity."

By late January 1866, even the pleasure of being praised throughout the country seemed to have worn off.

"Verily, all is vanity and little worth — save piloting," he wrote his mother and Pamela. "To think that after writing many an article a man might be excused for thinking tolerably good, those New York people should single out a villainous backwoods sketch to compliment me on! — 'Jim Smiley & His Jumping Frog' . . . "

The San Francisco police had been ordered to keep a close watch on him because of his anti-police articles, and two days after writing the letter, he was jailed overnight for being drunk in public.

Twain had earlier signed a contract with the Sacramento *Daily Union* to travel to the Sandwich Islands (later renamed the Hawaiian Islands) as their special correspondent. The *Daily Union* was sending him on the trip because increasing numbers of Californians wanted to invest in the islands' sugar, rice, and cotton industries. Twain's articles were seen as a way to bring together potential investors with the planters who were already there.

Mark Twain did his best to oblige, writing glowingly of the ready pool of cheap and reliable Chinese and Kanaka (Hawaiian for "man") labor. He recommended they be forced to work under rigid contract-labor laws, which were the kind of laws that strictly controlled the lives of black Americans in the South.

Twain seemed enchanted by the people, most of whom were "almost as dark as negroes," and admitted he was strongly attracted to the "dark, gingerbread colored beauties."

He defended the Hawaiians for killing the first European explorer to reach Hawaii, Captain James Cook, saying the killing was "justifiable homicide" because he repaid their kindnesses "with insult and ill-treatment."

Yet Twain also casually referred to the native Hawaiians as "savages." He had never before lived

Captain James Cook, the first European explorer to reach the Hawaiian Islands.

in a society where dark-skinned people were in the majority and exercised political power, however, and it forced him to examine his racial views.

Even though the native Hawaiians had already lost much of their land and power to whites from the United States and Europe, Twain's experiences in Hawaii — including seeing Hawaiian royalty — posed a challenge to his long-held belief in white superiority.

Twain often seemed to have good luck, and he experienced it again in Hawaii. A few days before starting the return trip to San Francisco, he heard that an open boat carrying fifteen starving men had drifted ashore on the island of Hawaii.

Their clipper ship, the *Hornet*, had burned to the waterline forty-three days before. The men were able to grab only a ten-day supply of food before abandoning ship, and had drifted 4,000 miles since then.

Twain was sick in bed at the time, but an American diplomat arranged for him to be carried to the hospital on a cot to interview the survivors. He worked through the night writing the story, then tossed it aboard a California-bound steamship in the morning.

His story of the incident was the first one to appear in the United States, and the *Daily Union* spread

The main Street of St. Louis, Missouri, in 1858.

it across three columns on the front page.

When Twain returned to California a few weeks later, he found he was "about the best-known honest man on the Pacific coast."

The owner of several theaters told him that now was the time to make his fortune on the lecture circuit, and he readily agreed.

But his first lecture was almost his last.

Fifteen hundred people showed up, and when he looked out at the huge throng "the fright which pervaded me from head to foot was paralyzing. It lasted two minutes and was as bitter as death; the memory of it is indestructible but it had its compensations, for it made me immune from timidity before audiences for all time to come."

The next day, one San Francisco paper said, "as a humorous writer Mark Twain stands in the foremost rank, while his effort of last evening affords reason for the belief that he can establish an equal reputation as a humorous and original lecturer."

More lectures followed throughout California and Nevada, including one to a packed audience in Virginia City. In one mining town, an old prospector who reluctantly agreed to introduce him grumbled: "Ladies and gentlemen, I know only two things about this man; the first is that he's never been in jail, and the second is I don't know why."

The lectures brought Twain several thousand dollars, even though creditors in Virginia City and Carson City attached part of the proceeds to cover old unpaid bills.

The lectures launched him on a career he would follow off and on for the rest of his life — a career that would one day rescue him from the financial ruin he dreaded.

In December, he sailed for New York as a roving correspondent for the *Alta California*. The ship almost sank during a fierce storm the first night out, but eventually arrived safely on the Pacific coast of Nicaragua.

Twain enjoyed the trip on the *America*, where he took an instant liking to the steamer's storytelling captain, Ned Wakeman, "with his strong, cheery voice, animated countenance, quaint phraseology, defiance of grammar, and extraordinary vim in the matter of gesture and emphasis . . . "

He recorded many of Wakeman's stories in his notebook, and would one day use the captain as the model for several fictional characters.

The passengers traveled across Nicaragua to the Atlantic side of the country, where a steamer was waiting to take them to New York.

On the journey north, the ship stopped briefly at Key West and Twain went ashore. Afterward, he wrote an article for the *Alta* saying lost sailors could find their way into Key West by following the smell of the black population.

That was the kind of "humor" Twain had learned

in Missouri and the West, but he would soon discover that many people in the East did not appreciate such comments.

The ship sailed safely into icy New York Harbor on January 12, and Twain looked around at the city he had last seen as a nineteen-year-old.

It was, he said, "a splendid desert — a domed and steepled solitude, where the stranger is lonely in the midst of a million of his race."

He spent the next few weeks sightseeing and looking up acquaintances from California and Nevada who had moved to New York. One of them was Charles Webb, founder and editor of *The Californian*.

Webb proposed collecting a group of Twain's sketches into a book, using the Jumping Frog story as the lead piece and the book's title. After a publisher turned down the idea, Webb said he would print the book himself and give Twain ten percent of the royalties.

At the beginning of March, Twain took the train to St. Louis to visit his mother and Pamela. While there he attended church with them several times a week and behaved so well he finally said, "I don't think I can stand it anymore."

But he stayed long enough to write a story for the *Alta* ridiculing women who petitioned the legislature for the right to vote. "It is time for all good men to tremble for their country," he declared.

After a month, he took a steamboat to Hannibal.

But though he was treated as a celebrity, he "found home a dreary place after my long absence; for half the children I had known were now wearing whiskers" and most of the adults he had known had died or moved away.

When he arrived back in New York, the first person he saw was John Murphy, the chief of the *Alta*'s New York bureau. For several months, Twain had been trying to persuade the editors to pay his passage on the first pleasure cruise from the United States to Europe and the Holy Land: the Holy Land Pleasure Excursion.

Now Murphy told him they had agreed, and would also pay him $20 for each article he sent back during the five-month excursion. The ship, the "stately-looking" *Quaker City*, was scheduled to sail June 8.

Twain was so excited, he dropped by the steamship office almost every day to see how preparations were going. He seemed much more excited over the trip than he was over the fact that Webb had just published his first book: *The Celebrated Jumping Frog of Calaveras County, and Other Sketches*.

The book received good reviews, but didn't sell well. Besides, Mark Twain said, it was "full of damnable errors of grammar and deadly inconsistencies of spelling . . . because I was away and did not read the proofs."

His schedule was busy as he tried to catch up on

articles he owed the *Alta*, but his friends made it even busier by demanding that he give at least one lecture.

Frank Fuller, who had been acting governor of Utah Territory in 1861, advised him to rent the biggest hall in the city because the people were "wild" to hear him.

Twain agreed, and on May 6 stepped onto the stage of Cooper Institute to find the seats, aisles, and even the stage packed with people.

He spoke about the Sandwich Islands for an hour and fifteen minutes, and the audience loved him. He made very little money from the lecture (thousands of tickets were given away because Twain feared few people would come), but he did receive "a working quantity of fame" from the appearance.

As time approached for the ship to sail, Twain grew more and more restless.

Several days before departure, he wrote his mother and Pamela, saying "I am wild with impatience to move — move — *move!* . . . Curse the endless delays! They always kill me — they make me neglect every duty & then I have a conscience that tears me like a wild beast. I wish I never had to stop *any-*where a month."

He was thirty-one years old and had been moving restlessly from place to place since leaving Hannibal fourteen years before. Now he was eager to move again, seeking both the peace and the excitement he seemed to need as much as food and water.

The excitement would come on the journey that would take him to countries he had read about and dreamed of as a child. And eventually, because of a photograph shown him by a fellow passenger on the shore of the Aegean Sea, much peace would come as well.

7

THE MOST BEAUTIFUL
GIRL I EVER SAW

There were over sixty other passengers on the ship, including several clergymen and their parishioners. These "pilgrims," whose main purpose in taking the trip was to see the Holy Land, started singing psalms while they were still within sight of Brooklyn.

Twain quickly made friends with eight or nine like-minded young men, who had little interest in singing psalms. Their activities included smoking, drinking, and playing cards.

Twain also helped form a debating society, and jotted down possible debating subjects in his notebook, including: "Is a tail absolutely necessary to the comfort & convenience of a dog? — & if so would not a multiplicity of tails augment the dog's comfort & convenience by a constantly increasing ratio until his ability to carry them was exhausted?"

One of the passengers was a seventeen-year-old from Elmira, New York, named Charles Jervis Langdon. His wealthy parents had sent him abroad to keep him out of trouble.

Twain didn't have much to do with him at first,

saying he was "pleasant, & well meaning, but fearful green & fearfully slow . . . "

Though Twain didn't know it yet, "Charley" would turn out to be one of the most important people in his life.

Another person Twain befriended was Mrs. Mary Fairbanks, an experienced journalist. She was just

Charles Jervis Langdon, "Charley," (right) destined to become Twain's brother-in-law.

six years older, but he called her "Mother" and listened as she urged him to stop using slang (dialect and raw humor) in his writings and speech. He allowed her to edit his letters to the *Alta*.

One day Twain crumpled up some pages and threw them away, telling a fellow passenger: "Well, Mrs. Fairbanks has just destroyed another four hours' work for me."

The *Quaker City* stopped briefly in the Azores, then headed for Gibraltar.

Twain was impressed to find that the Moroccan consul to Gibraltar was a black man who had purchased his freedom and "become so smart & well posted in Gib[raltar] affairs the Emperor gave him his master's place & he has held it for years."

In spite of the man's impressive credentials, though, Twain referred to him in his notebook as "Nigger Consul."

Most of the *Quaker City* passengers headed north toward Paris after the Gibraltar stopover, but Twain and four others decided to go to Tangiers, Morocco, to be "among the Africans, Moors, Arabs & Bedouins of the desert."

It turned out to be one of the highlights of the excursion.

"I would not give this experience for all the balance of the trip combined," he wrote his mother and Pamela. The buildings and dress of the people were "strange beyond description," and there was "not the slightest thing that we have seen save in pictures and we always mistrusted the pictures before. We cannot any more. The pictures used to seem . . . too fanciful for reality. But, behold, they were not wild enough."

He was fascinated by the different skin colors of the people, including "original, genuine negroes, as black as Moses," and "the five thousand Jews in blue gaberdines, sashes about their waists, slippers upon their feet . . . they are an inconceivably rusty-looking set now and consequently must have been in the days of the Old Testament."

His *Alta* letter about Tangiers contained a depth and lyricism his writing had never possessed before, as if he had suddenly discovered — in this land of ancient structures and ancient people — a beauty and a mystery he had never known before.

Twain and his friends bought flowing robes, fezzes, and yellow slippers, which they wore at a shipboard ball as the *Quaker City* headed for France.

He was already getting restless again, and when they arrived at Marseilles "we had no disposition to examine carefully into anything at all — we only wanted to glance and go — to move and keep moving!"

He seemed to grow more and more restless as the excursion continued, and more and more angry at the poverty he saw.

In Paris he visited the Louvre and saw "miles" of

paintings by old masters whose "nauseous adulation of princely patrons was more prominent to me and chained my attention more surely than the charms of color and expression which are claimed to be in the pictures."

He thought the palace of Versailles was "wonderfully beautiful!" and enjoyed watching the wild can-can being danced by women who lifted their dresses as high as possible. ("I placed my hands before my face for very shame. But I looked through my fingers.")

But then he visited a neighborhood filled with crime and with desperately poor people, and declared that "misery, poverty, vice and crime go hand in hand, and the evidences of it stare one in the face from every side. Here the people live who begin the revolutions."

Italy brought out his admiration and anger even more. Most of all, however, he felt outrage at the desperation of the poor, in contrast to the wealth and privilege enjoyed by church officials and royalty.

In Venice, as in Tangiers, he was confronted with a black man who challenged his belief that black people were inferior to whites.

The only guide the *Quaker City* passengers had who knew anything, according to Twain, was a black man from South Carolina whose parents had been slaves. He read and spoke four languages fluently, and knew the history of Venice by heart.

"He dresses better than any of us, I think, and is daintily polite," Twain said. "Negroes are deemed as good as white people, in Venice, and so this man feels no desire to go back to his native land. His judgment is correct."

From Italy, the passengers sailed to Greece, where officials said they would have to stay in quarantine several days before they could land. That night Twain and three others rowed ashore in a small boat and made their way on foot to the Acropolis.

A full moon shone on "a world of ruined sculpture" that lay around them. Looking down from the top of the hill, they saw "a vision! And such a vi-

The Greek Isles, "a world of ruined sculpture."

sion! Athens by moonlight! The prophet that thought the splendors of the New Jerusalem were revealed to him, surely saw this instead!"

From Greece they sailed to Turkey, and then on to Yalta, Russia, to visit Czar Alexander II at his summer palace.

The *Quaker City* finally sailed back down to Turkey, then to Beirut, Lebanon. There Twain and seven others separated from the main party and took a three-week trip through the Holy Land on horseback.

He was horrified by the poverty, ignorance, and desolation he found.

Nazareth consisted of "dirt and rags and squalor; vermin, hunger and wretchedness; savage costumes, savage weapons and looks of hate — these are the things that meet one at every step in Nazareth."

The only place that felt right to him was the Hill of Calvary, where he "gazed upon the place where the true cross once stood, with a far more absorbing interest than I ever felt in anything earthly before."

He left the hill, walked to a small shop, and bought a Bible for his mother.

But the reality of squalid villages, widespread hatred, and children "in all stages of mutilation and decay," made him thankful when the trip was over.

The excursion's final stop before heading back toward the United States was Egypt.

Twain climbed to the top of the Pyramid of Cheops,

a vast structure that made the mountain of his Hannibal childhood — Holliday's Hill — seem as nothing in comparison.

But it was the Sphinx that brought out the same awe he had felt standing before the ancient wall in Tangiers. Watching the 189-foot-long sculpture gazing out "over the ocean of Time — over lines of century-waves," Twain said the vast figure made him think of "everyone who longs for the people and places of the past."

The trip was now nearing its end. Though Twain didn't know it, one of the most important moments of his life had occurred off the coast of Turkey a few weeks earlier.

One afternoon while the ship lay at anchor in the Bay of Smyrna, Charley Langdon invited him into his cabin, as he often did. Usually on such occasions, Charley displayed his latest souvenirs, but this time he showed Twain a miniature portrait of his older sister.

Her name was Olivia and she was twenty-two years old.

"He looked at it with long admiration, and spoke of it reverently, for the delicate face seemed to him to be something more than a mere human likeness," a friend wrote of Twain's reaction.

"Each time he came, after that, he asked to see the picture, and once even begged to be allowed to take it away with him. The boy would not agree to this,

The miniature portrait of Olivia Langdon, whom Twain resolved he would marry.

and the elder man looked long and steadily at the miniature, resolving in his mind that some day he would meet the owner of that lovely face. . . . ”

The *Quaker City* returned to New York on November 19, 1867, and Twain was the first passenger ashore. He spent only two days in the city, then hurried to Washington, D.C., to become private secretary to Senator William Stewart of Nevada.

“If I lecture *now*,” he wrote Frank Fuller, who was urging him to accept several dates, “I shall have to do it solely on the *Quaker City*’s fame, & take many, *very many* chances — chances that might utterly damn me. If I stay here all winter & keep . . . getting well acquainted with great dignitaries to introduce me . . . I can lecture next season on my *own* reputation, to 100 houses, & houses that will be readier to accept me without criticism than they are now.

"I have to make a bran[d] new start in the lecturing business, & I don't mean to do it in Tuttletown, Ark, or Baldwinsville, Michigan, either."

He also wanted to be in Washington so he could secure a political appointment for Orion who, as usual, was on the brink of financial ruin.

But while Mark Twain was offered jobs, no one was interested in Orion. Less than a month after arriving in Washington, Twain told Fuller he was "already dead tired of being in one place so long."

In addition, he and Senator Stewart had a falling out when Twain told some constituents they could use "a nice substantial jail and a free school" more than the post office they were requesting. "If any letters came there, you couldn't read them," he said.

He wrote a humorous and exaggerated account of his parting with the senator, saying that when Stewart bellowed, " 'Leave the house! Leave it forever and forever, too!,' [I] regarded that as a sort of covert intimation that my services would be dispensed with, and so I resigned."

There was also talk that he had helped himself too freely to the senator's whiskey and cigars.

Twain traveled to New York to spend the Christmas holidays with friends and, on New Year's Day, visited the Langdon family. He arrived about 11:00 A.M., intending to stay an hour, but stayed thirteen hours.

It was the first time he had seen Olivia in person, and he would never forget the experience.

"She was slender and beautiful and girlish — and she was both girl and woman," he remembered almost forty years later. "She remained both girl and woman to the last day of her life."

He felt that she was even more beautiful than her portrait, and far above him socially and economically. He told his mother that Livy was small and frail, and to Mother Fairbanks he wrote: "There isn't much of her, but what there is assays as high as any bullion that ever I saw."

Elisha Bliss of the American Publishing Company had written Twain within days of his return from abroad, asking him to write a travel book based on his *Quaker City* letters.

Twain had received requests from several other publishers for such a book, but said "I had made up my mind to *one* thing — I wasn't going to touch a book unless there was *money* in it, & a good deal of it."

Bliss's company published books by subscription, which meant they sent door-to-door salesmen out to solicit orders. If there were enough orders to ensure a profit, the book was published, but if there were not enough orders, the book was not published. All of the books were thick and handsomely bound in order to make them more attractive to customers.

Though subscription publishing was looked down on by "respectable" publishers, the profit potential for an author was great because of the large number of salesmen pushing a book.

Bliss offered Twain $10,000 or five percent of the royalties. Twain was almost broke and was tempted to take the money, but he turned it down and signed a contract for the royalties. It was, he often said, "the best business judgment I ever displayed."

He was still faced with the problem of making a living, however, and he solved the problem by joining with a friend to form the country's first newspaper syndicate.

They made $24 a week by selling letters on politics in Washington at $2 apiece to twelve newspapers "all scattered far away among the back settlements." Unfortunately, his partner was a heavy drinker.

The $24 would have really been riches, Twain said, "if we hadn't had to support that jug."

The next few months were a whirlwind of turning out articles for the newspapers, lecturing throughout the country, and trying to write the 500-to-600-page book he had promised Bliss.

Twain panicked when he learned that the *Alta* editors had copyrighted his *Quaker City* letters to them, and planned to publish their own book.

He had written the *Alta* letters primarily for his unsophisticated Western audience of miners, workingmen, and others who appreciated the coarse humor he had perfected as a reporter. Now he wanted to prove to a wider audience, including the clergymen, intellectuals, and other educated people he was meeting in the East, that he should be taken seriously as an author.

"If the *Alta*'s book were to come out with those wretched, slangy letters unrevised, I should be utterly ruined," he declared.

Bliss loaned him the money to take a steamer to San Francisco, where he persuaded the *Alta* owners to drop their book plans.

He then went on a lecture tour in California and Nevada, including stops in Virginia City and Carson City, where he was greeted like a conquering hero.

Returning to San Francisco, he wrote most of his book in two months by working "every night from eleven or twelve until broad day in the morning, averaging more than three thousand words a day."

He delivered his manuscript to Bliss near the end of July, and later spent two weeks with the Langdons in Elmira.

He and "Livy" (as everyone called Olivia), spent their days taking carriage rides, strolling in the garden of the Langdons' mansion, and singing around

Portrait of Olivia Clemens in 1869, the year she and Mark Twain married.

the piano. Livy's mother and a visiting cousin were usually with them.

The Langdons, who were founders of a local church, said prayers and sang hymns every evening. There was nothing stronger to drink in the house than cider, and they didn't believe in smoking.

It was, to say the least, not the kind of lifestyle Mark Twain was used to. He enjoyed himself, though, and was fascinated by Livy. Her cousin saw that he was falling in love, so she left Elmira "thinking the courtship might progress better if I were out of the way."

Near the end of the visit, he worked up the nerve to propose to Livy, but she turned him down. She also refused to give him a photograph, but finally agreed to be his "sister."

Even before Twain left the house, he wrote a letter calling her "My Honored 'Sister.'"

"Give me a little room in that great heart of yours — only the little you have promised me — & if I fail to deserve it may I remain forever the homeless vagabond I am!"

He spent the next few months lecturing and working on his book, but also found time to keep asking Livy to marry him. She turned him down every time, though she had taken to affectionately calling him "Youth," perhaps seeing the wayward child that would always be a part of him.

Once while visiting a friend in New York, tears came into his eyes as he talked about how Livy was too high above him to ever say yes.

His friend raced over and embraced him, declaring: "Go for her, and get her, and God bless you, Sam!"

Twain looked at him in surprise, then promised to "harass that girl and harass her till she'll *have* to say yes!"

His persistence paid off in late November when she agreed to marry him if her parents approved. That was far from certain, for while the Langdons liked Twain as a visitor, they had definite reservations about him as a potential son-in-law.

"I have learned from Charlie & I think the same idea has pervaded your conversation, or writing or both," Mrs. Langdon wrote to Twain's fellow *Quaker City* passenger, Mother Fairbanks, "that a great change had taken place in Mr. Clemens, that he seemed to have entered upon a new manner of life, with higher & better purposes actuating his conduct.

"The question, the answer to which, would settle a most weaning anxiety, is, — from what standard of conduct, — from what habitual life, did this change, or improvement, or reformation; commence?"

At about the same time, Twain tried to convince Livy's mother that whatever he may have done in the past, "I now claim that I am a Christian."

In a letter to Mother Fairbanks, he promised "to seek the society of the good — I shall be a *Christian*. I shall climb — climb — climb toward this bright sun that is shining in the heaven of my happiness. . . . "

Mrs. Fairbanks praised Twain in her reply to Olivia's mother, but she was the only one who did.

Mr. Langdon had asked for references from Twain, and he gave the names of several men in California and Nevada, including at least two clergymen and a Sunday school superintendent.

But the replies weren't at all what Twain wanted.

One man said, "Clemens is a humbug . . . a man who has talent no doubt, but will make trivial use of it," while a second predicted he would "fill a pauper's grave." A third said he would "fill a drunkard's grave," while a fourth declared that he was "born to be hung."

"Haven't you any friend that you could suggest?" Mr. Langdon asked him.

"Apparently none whose testimony would be valuable," a somber Twain replied.

Mr. Langdon held out his hand and said, "You have at least one. *I* believe in you. I know you better than *they* do."

Mark and Livy became engaged on February 4, 1869, but in the months that followed, he was often on the road lecturing, or in Hartford reading the proofs of his book.

He also spent several weeks in Elmira, where Livy helped him with the editing, a task she would perform for the rest of her life.

The book, *The Innocents Abroad*, was published in July. It delighted American readers with its debunking of the glories of European civilization, and established Twain's reputation as an author. By the end of August it had sold over 5,000 copies and been acclaimed by critics throughout the country.

One of Twain's favorite reviews appeared in the prestigious *Atlantic Monthly*. It was written by a young novelist and editor named William Dean Howells, who would later become one of his best friends.

Howells said the book contained a large amount of

*A drawing of
Mark Twain writing*
The Innocents Abroad.

"pure human nature, such as rarely gets into literature," and called Twain an original genius who was "quite worthy of the company of the best."

Livy was pleased with this recognition of his broader talents, because she hated to see him described simply as a "humorist."

"Poor girl," Twain wrote Mrs. Fairbanks, "anybody who could convince her that I was not a humorist would secure her eternal gratitude!"

"I want the public . . . to know something of his deeper, larger nature," Livy Langdon said. "I remember being quite incensed by a lady's asking, 'Is there anything of Mr. Clemens except his humor?' "

Twain was equally defensive about his reputation

as a humorist, and hoped that people would see beyond his jokes to his deeper observations about humanity.

Several months earlier, he had told Livy: *"Don't read a word in that Jumping Frog book, Livy — don't. I hate to hear that infamous volume mentioned. I would be glad to know that every copy of it was burned, & gone forever."*

The struggle to be accepted for the serious things he wrote would last for the rest of his life.

On February 2, 1870, Mark and Livy were married in the living room of the Langdons' home. His new wife, Mark wrote a friend, was the "most beautiful girl I ever saw . . . & the sweetest . . . " Her father's

The house in Buffalo, New York, given to Livy by her father.

wedding gift was a house in Buffalo, complete with furnishings, household servants, a carriage, and a horse.

Over a year earlier, after Livy finally agreed to marry him, Mark told her the beginning of the year had "found me a waif, floating at random upon the sea of life, & it leaves me freighted with a good purpose, & blessed with a fair wind, a chart to follow, a port to reach. . . . It found me ready to welcome any wind that would blow my vagrant bark abroad, no matter where — it leaves me seeking home & an anchorage, & longing for them."

At last the lonely wandering of his youth was over.

8

THE MISTS OF THE PAST

Twain could hardly have married into a family more different from his own.

His family was poor, while the Langdons were rich. His family had been slaveowners, while the Langdons fought to end slavery.

During the Civil War, while Twain was defending slavery or keeping silent about it, the Langdons were sheltering runaway slaves in their home. There was even a secret tunnel used to hide runaways, leading from their home to the anti-slavery church that they helped found across the street.

The country's leading abolitionists were their friends, and Frederick Douglass — the great black leader and abolitionist — was a welcome visitor to their home.

In San Francisco, Twain had written angry articles about the mistreatment of Chinese, but continued to write derogatory articles about black people. In the last two years before his marriage to Livy Langdon, however, he had begun to modify his racial views.

In a January 1867 letter to the *Alta*, he changed "nigger" to "negro," and carefully made the same changes in the final proofs of *The Innocents Abroad*.

His desire to be accepted by Livy and her parents undoubtedly helped this process along. It was also speeded up by the fact that many of the people he was now becoming friends with had been leaders in the fight to abolish slavery and would not accept him if he was openly anti-black.

But his changing racial views also had a deeper foundation. He had expressed anger at injustices toward the powerless many times, and now that anger was being extended to include those who were powerless because of the color of their skin.

It would still take years for him to overcome the destructive racial attitudes he had been taught. But the sense he had as a child that the treatment of black Americans was wrong — even though churches, schools, courts, and his parents approved of that treatment — was once again stirring within him.

A few months before his marriage, Mr. Langdon loaned him money to buy a one-third interest in the Buffalo *Express*, and one of the first articles he wrote was a searing condemnation of the lynching of a black man in Tennessee for raping a white woman. The man was later found to be innocent.

His outrage at lynching, and the so-called sense of chivalry of Southern white males that justified lynching, would burn within him the rest of his life.

"A little blunder in the administration of justice by

Southern mob law, but nothing to speak of . . . , " he wrote. "But mistakes will happen, even in the conduct of the best regulated and most high toned mobs, and surely there is no good reason why Southern gentlemen should worry themselves with useless regrets, so long as only an innocent 'nigger' is hanged, or roasted or knouted to death, now and then. . . . "

A few weeks later he included the following item in a column: "Another trifling mistake by Judge Lynch: The negro found hanging near Dresden, Tennessee, a few years ago, and who was supposed to have been hung for committing a rape on a small girl, has proved not to be the right person."

These denunciations were forerunners to the powerful condemnation of lynchers he would make in *Huckleberry Finn.*

Livy's father died in August and Livy, who was always frail, became seriously ill. In November, their first child was born prematurely. Langdon, as they named him, was also frail and had to be nursed constantly. Twain was so exhausted by the round-the-clock tending of his wife and son, and worry about their survival, he wondered if he was losing both his creative powers and his sanity.

"Sometimes I have hope for my wife," he said, " — so I have at this moment — but most of the time it seems to me impossible that she can get well."

*Langdon Clemens,
Twain's first child,
1870–1872.*

And to Orion, he wrote, "I am still nursing Livy night and day. I am nearly worn out."

But in the midst of this dark time, during the winter of 1870–71, he found a way to join his gift for humor with his anger at injustice in a more powerful way than ever.

In several articles written for the *Express* and a magazine called the *Galaxy*, he used the "half-insane tempests and cyclones of humor" that were assaulting him in his depression to denounce racism, corruption in Congress, the immorality of big business, and religious hypocrisy (calling one minister a "crawling, slimy, sanctimonious, self-righteous reptile!" for refusing to allow an actor to be buried from his church).

These articles were his farewell to journalism as a career, and he was glad to say good-bye.

In April 1871, Twain sold his interest in the *Express* at a loss, put the house up for sale, and moved with his wife and son to Quarry Farm just outside Elmira.

Quarry Farm, which belonged to Livy's sister, would be the scene of his most prolific writing in the years to come. For the present, though, they planned to stay only a few weeks before moving to Hartford.

Twain continued to worry that he had lost much of his writing ability. A few months earlier he signed a contract with Bliss to write another 600-page book, this time about his experiences in the West. Twain wanted it to be called *The Innocents at Home*, but Bliss said it should be called *Roughing It*. The writing went slowly, and Twain was certain it wasn't good.

When Joe Goodman came to the farm for a visit, Twain handed him the manuscript to read.

"Joe," he said, "I guess I'm done for . . . I'm afraid I'll never be able to reach the standard of *The Innocents Abroad* again. Here is what I have written, Joe. Read it, and see if that is your opinion."

Goodman read silently for several minutes while Twain pretended to write. Finally he could stand it no longer and threw down his pen.

"I knew it! I knew it!" he exclaimed. "I am writing nothing but rot. . . . I have been trying to write a funny book, with dead people and sickness everywhere. . . . Oh, Joe, I wish to God I could die myself!"

"I have found it perfectly absorbing," Goodman replied. "You are doing a great book!"

Twain was overjoyed, and spent the rest of the summer completing the book. During the summer, he and Livy also found out she was pregnant again. They wanted a home of their own where they could raise their family, and discussed where that home should be.

The house in Hartford, Connecticut, where Mark Twain wrote some of his most famous works.

Hartford was their choice, and they moved there in October. Except for trips abroad and summers at Quarry Farm, Hartford would be their home for the next 20 years.

Twain had to leave almost immediately on a lecture tour, even though he had said over two years earlier: "I most cordially hate the lecture field. And after all, I shudder to think I may never get out of it."

But lecturing was the quickest and easiest way he had found to make money, and he would be forced into it the rest of his life. He completed the tour in February just as *Roughing It* was published, muttering that if he ever lectured again for less than $500, he would "be pretty hungry."

The sales and reviews of *Roughing It* were good, and the writing showed that he was learning to do more than simply relate his experiences in a humorous way — he was now able to exaggerate and dramatize them so they were even more powerful as fiction than as fact.

Further lifting his spirits was the birth in March of his second child, Olivia Susan. "Susy," as they called her, would often remind him of himself in the years to come.

In June, the grief they thought they had left behind found them again. Nineteen-month-old Langdon died, and Twain blamed himself, though he was ashamed to tell anyone what happened until almost forty years later.

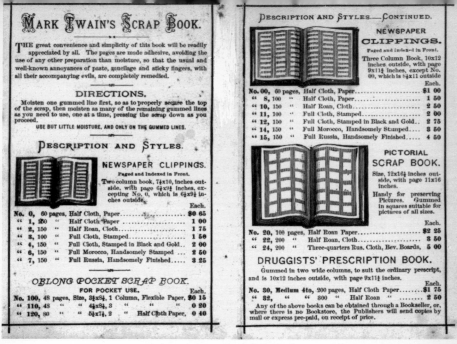

Mark Twain's first invention.

Taking his son for a ride in an open carriage, he said he "dropped into a reverie and forgot all about my charge. The furs fell away and exposed his bare legs. . . . The child was almost frozen. I hurried home with him. I was aghast at what I had done and feared the consequences. I have always felt shame for that treacherous morning's work. . . ."

Later in the summer, Twain came out with the first of many inventions that would take so much of his time and, eventually, so much of his and Livy's money and happiness. He called his first invention the "Mark Twain Scrap-Book."

During the latter part of the 1800s, people had to use paste to glue items into their scrapbooks, and it was usually a messy process. Twain invented a scrapbook that had narrow strips of gum that were moistened with a sponge, which allowed the item to easily be pressed onto the page. The scrapbook sold well for several years, but his partner took most of the profits.

In August, Mark left for the first of many trips to England, and stayed almost three months. Much of his time was spent successfully trying to gain copyright protection for *Roughing It* (one English publisher had made a small fortune reprinting his writings without permission), and in taking notes for a book on England that he would never write.

Most of all, however, he was stunned and almost overwhelmed by the fame and adulation that greeted him in England.

"He was shy as a girl . . . and could hardly be coaxed to meet the learned and great who wanted to take him by the hand," said one man.

Twain told Mrs. Fairbanks that "the really great ones are very easy to get along with, even when hampered with titles. But I will confess that mediocrity with a title is (to me) a formidable thing to encounter — it don't talk & I'm afraid to."

But to Livy, he wrote proudly: "I have been received in a sort of tremendous way to-night by the brains of London . . . mine being (between you and me) a name which was received with a thundering outburst of spontaneous applause. . . . "

Now, for the first time, he saw himself as an author. Where once he had mined for silver and gold, now he would mine the past and find what was most valuable in it for himself and others.

One evening in the winter of 1873, Mark and Livy sat conversing with their close friends and neighbors, Charles and Susan Warner. Charles was publisher of the Hartford *Courant*, a travel writer for *Harper's Magazine*, and a novelist.

The talk turned to the novels their wives were reading, and when Mark and Charles criticized their quality, Livy and Susan challenged them to write a better one. It was a challenge neither could refuse.

They agreed to collaborate, and Twain began working right away. He wrote the first eleven chapters, while Warner wrote the next twelve. The sixty-three-chapter book was finished two months later, with Twain doing slightly more than half the writing.

They wrote the book, he said, "in the superstition that we were writing one coherent yarn, when I suppose, as a matter of fact, we were writing two *in*coherent ones."

The book was *The Gilded Age*, and its name is still a synonym for the political and economic corruption of that era, when congressmen and businessmen stole immense sums from "the great putty-hearted public."

Few other writers had been critical of the corruption of the era, with its robber barons plundering the U.S. Treasury and senators selling their votes for as much as $10,000 apiece.

Twain and Warner were denounced by a majority of the reviewers for their harsh criticism of government and business practices, with one saying they should have written about "the pleasanter features of American life."

Other reviewers questioned whether "a mere comic like Mark Twain" was capable of writing a serious novel, and said that Warner had probably done all the writing.

The leading character in *The Gilded Age* is Colonel Beriah Sellers, a Southern "gentleman" with one get-rich-quick scheme after another. His latest scheme is to sell some barren Tennessee land to the government for millions of dollars, ostensibly so a university can be built for black people.

Sellers, modeled after a cousin of Twain's named James Lampton, enlists the aid of Senator Abner Dilworthy (modeled after Samuel C. Pomeroy, a corrupt senator from Kansas that Twain despised). Dilworthy spouts Sunday school pieties while lining his pockets with bribes.

But in some ways the book's most fascinating character is Laura Hawkins. Named after Twain's childhood friend, she is an ambitious and manipulative woman whose dream is "to be rich; she wanted luxury, she wanted men at her feet, her slaves."

Throughout his career, Twain was much better at portraying males than females. Most fiction writers of the times presented young women as charming, innocent, and almost childishly incapable of taking care of themselves.

Twain increasingly tried to show women in more realistic ways, as he did with Laura. He failed more often than he succeeded, but he was keenly aware of the need to write about them more honestly. Ironically, the most completely real woman in any of his books was a racially mixed woman: Roxana, the heroine in *Pudd'nhead Wilson*, a novel about interracial crime and punishment.

The Gilded Age was an immediate hit with the public, and sold out three printings the first month. Twain was in England when the book came out. He had to be there the day the English edition of *The Gilded Age* was published, in order to protect the British copyright.

Livy and Susy went with him and stayed for several months, with Livy becoming increasingly homesick. There were delays in printing the book, and they weren't sure when it would be published.

"I would not hesitate [to stay] *one moment* if it were simply for the money that his copyright will bring him," a homesick Livy wrote her sister, "but if his reputation will be better for his staying and lecturing, of course he ought to stay. . . . The truth is, I can't bear the thought of postponing going home."

Susy Clemens, Twain's second child, at the age of 6.

Mark and Livy were having a new home built in Hartford, and Livy was also anxious to see how that was progressing.

One night when they returned to their hotel from the theater, they were stunned to learn that bankers had stopped payment on their account. The speculation he and Warner had written about in *The Gilded*

Age had caused the collapse of their banking firm, Jay Cooke and Company.

The couple lay awake all night worrying about what to do. Mark felt guilty about not withdrawing their money earlier, and finally told Livy he could lecture to "get money to pay our debts and get us home."

"Lecturing is what Mr. C.[lemens] always speaks of doing when their [sic] seems any need of money," Livy wrote.

They sailed home in October, but Twain was back in England a month later to await publication of the book and to give several well-paid lectures. In addition to their problems with the bank, the house was costing a lot more than they expected.

It was the most elaborate house in Hartford, with 19 rooms, 5 baths, Gothic turrets, a balcony shaped like a pilothouse, and a porch shaped like a riverboat deck.

In January 1874, Mark wrote Livy that he would be sailing for home in a few days.

"I love to write about arriving . . . ," he told her. "And I love to picture myself ringing the bell, at midnight — then a pause of a second or two — then the turning of the bolt, & 'Who is it?'—then ever so many kisses . . . I do love & honor you, my darling."

Livy was pregnant again, and the next few weeks were spent preparing for the birth of their third child. She almost suffered a miscarriage and was confined

Twain's third child, Clara Clemens, at the age of 4.

to bed, but when she was well enough they traveled to Quarry Farm.

On June 8, 1874, Clara Langdon Clemens was born there. She weighed almost eight pounds, and Twain called her "the great American Giantress."

His sister-in-law, Susan Crane, had a study built

for him on a small hill far from the house, where he could work without being disturbed.

It was an eight-sided room with a large glass window in each side, and Twain said that "when the storms sweep down the remote valley and the lightning flashes above the hills beyond, and the rain beats upon the roof over my head, imagine the luxury of it!"

He was now starting the routine he would follow the next several years: spending the summers writing in the study at Quarry Farm, and relaxing and entertaining friends in Hartford the rest of the year.

A few days after his marriage four years earlier, he had written to his childhood friend and fellow riverboat pilot, Will Bowen:

"The old life has swept before me like a panorama; the old days have trooped by in their old glory again; the old faces have looked out of the mists of the past; old footsteps have sounded in my listening ears; old hands have clasped mine, and the songs I loved ages and ages ago have come wailing down the centuries. . . . "

A few months afterward, he wrote Livy that "down in my heart of hearts I yearn for the days that are gone and the phantoms of olden time."

Now, at the age of 38, he reached back into the old life of Hannibal and the days that were gone to begin writing his first great dream of the past: *The Adventures of Tom Sawyer*.

Throughout the summer he worked on the manuscript, which he would later call "a hymn put into prose to give it a worldly air."

Some days he wrote fifty pages, but by the end of the summer his enthusiasm and ideas had run dry, so he laid the manuscript aside. This would become his usual way of working on books — periods of intense writing, followed by intervals of working on something else or not writing at all.

"It is my habit to keep four or five books in process of erection all the time and every summer add a few courses of bricks to two or three of them," he said several years later, "but I cannot forecast which of the two or three it is going to be."

One evening while sitting on the porch at Quarry Farm, he listened to the Langdons' black cook tell about her past. She had been born into slavery in the South, was sold twice, and had seen her husband and seven children sold from an auction block.

She searched for her family for 13 years, and was finally reunited with one of her sons — the only family member she ever saw again.

Twain wrote a three-page sketch called "A True Story," based on what she told him. He made no mention of his family's slave-holding past, or of being raised in a slave society. Instead, he portrayed the narrator as a Northerner who was shocked to discover how brutal slavery had been.

Twain then turned the story over to the black cook, whom he called Aunt Rachel, and presented the longest uninterrupted monologue he would give to a black person in any of his writings. The result was powerful.

Though Twain attributed a stereotyped "Negro dialect" to her and portrayed her as believing in all kinds of superstitions (including many he would later attribute to Jim in *Huckleberry Finn*), the story was a devastating indictment of slavery.

Aunt Rachel told how she stood on an auction block and watched as her husband was sold, and then six of her children. When there was only one child left, she warned she'd kill the man that touched him.

"But dey got him — dey got him, de men did; but I took and tear de cloe's mos' off of 'em an' beat 'em over de head wid my chain; an' *dey* give it to *me*, too, but I didn't mine dat.

"Well, dah was my ole man gone, an' all my chil'en . . . an' six of 'em I hain't set eyes on ag'n to dis day, an' dat's twenty-two year ago las' Easter."

Though "A True Story" was written at a time when the contributions of blacks in the Civil War were already being denied or ignored, and the ex-slaves were being described as less than human, Mark Twain told how Aunt Rachel was finally found by a son in a black Union Army regiment who had searched for her throughout the South.

Howells published "A True Story" in the prestigious *Atlantic*, in November 1874, marking another milestone in Twain's acceptance by the Eastern intellectuals he was so eager to impress.

But not everyone was pleased with the story.

"Mark Twain can be so very funny," wrote one critic after reading it, "that we are naturally as dissatisfied with him, when he is not funny at all, as we should be with a parrot that could not talk, or a rose that had no odor."

Mark and Livy moved into their new home in October, even though it was still unfinished. Howells asked him for another story for the *Atlantic*, but Twain wrote him a letter saying he was "in such a state of worry and confusion that my head won't go."

A few minutes after mailing the letter, he went walking with his friend, Reverend Joseph Twichell, pastor of Hartford's Asylum Hill Congregational Church (because of its wealthy parishioners, Twain called it the Church of the Holy Speculators).

Two hours after writing the first letter, Twain sent Howells a second letter. "I take back the remark that I can't write for the January number," he said, "for Twichell and I have had a long walk in the woods, and I got to telling him about old Mississippi days of steamboating glory and grandeur as I saw them (during four years) *from the pilot-house*. He said, 'What a virgin subject to hurl into a magazine!' I hadn't thought of that before. Would you like a series of papers to run through 3 months or 6 or 9 — or about 4 months, say?"

Howells was delighted with the idea, and Twain quickly sent off the first article.

"The piece about the Mississippi is capital," Howells wrote back. "It almost made the water in our ice-pitcher muddy as I read it."

And so, in the latter part of 1874 and the first few months of 1875, Mark Twain wrote what would turn out to be the first part of *Life on the Mississippi* — a book he hadn't planned and would not finish for eight more years.

Though he didn't know it, he was now at the beginning of the happiest and most productive period of his life.

9

BEST BOY STORY
I EVER READ

Mark and Livy's home was on a one-hundred-acre, wooded tract called Nook Farm, which was the literary and social center of Hartford.

Their next-door neighbor was Harriet Beecher Stowe, the author of *Uncle Tom's Cabin*, while another neighbor was her sister, Isabella Beecher Hooker, an ardent feminist who founded the New England Woman Suffrage Association in 1868.

Charles Dudley Warner and his wife lived nearby, as did J. Hammond Trumbull, the most learned man in Hartford. Twain especially admired him because he could swear in twenty-seven languages.

Joe Twichell and his wife, Harmony, were also neighbors and regular visitors to the house, where Twain relished his role as host and entertainer.

"M.T. *never* was so funny as this time," Twichell wrote after one dinner. "The perfect art of a certain kind of story telling will die with him."

One evening, Twain suddenly stood up and began singing spirituals in his soft tenor. One of the songs was "Nobody Knows the Trouble I've Seen," and when he came to the end he gave a great shout of "Glory, Glory, Hallelujah!" Those present said they would remember the performance as long as they lived.

Another evening, he seemed transported to some distant time and place as he sang one spiritual after another: "He swayed gently as he stood; his voice was low and soft, a whisper of wind in the trees; his eyes were closed, and he smiled strangely."

Twain loved the companionship of his New England friends, especially Joe Twichell.

Twichell was athletic, and Twain decided that he was, too. When a walking craze swept the country, they took ten-mile hikes. When a bicycling craze followed that, they bought the high-wheelers that became so popular. Twain also loved spectator sports, including baseball. Once, when a boy stole his umbrella at a game, Mark offered a five-dollar reward for the return of the umbrella and a two hundred-dollar reward for the return of the boy's remains.

Spelling bees at Twichell's church were also one of his favorite pastimes, but he possessed unique ideas about spelling.

"I don't see any use in having a uniform and arbitrary way of spelling words," he told one audience. "We might as well make all clothes alike and cook all dishes alike. . . . Kow spelled with a large K is just as good as with a small one. It is better. . . . It suggests to the mind a grand, vague, impressive new kind of a cow."

Livy worked on "improving" Mark, including persuading him to say grace and read the Bible at meals, and cut out drinking, smoking, and swearing. The results were promising, but temporary.

Grace was the first to go. In fact, it never even made it out of Buffalo. Joe Goodman visited Mark and Livy a few months after they were married, and said the worst shock of his life was seeing Twain say grace and read the Bible.

"You may keep this up," Mark finally told Livy, "if you want to, but I must ask you to excuse me from it. It is making me a hypocrite. I don't believe in this Bible. It contradicts my reason."

Smoking and drinking quickly followed.

His attempts not to swear lasted the longest of the "reforms," at least as far as Livy knew. Mark claimed that for ten years he did his swearing in private, usually in the bathroom next to his and Livy's bedroom.

But one Sunday morning, he neglected to totally close the door, and that was his undoing.

His shirts were made especially for him, with an opening in the back secured by a button at the top. He put on a shirt, discovered the button was missing, and angrily threw the shirt out the window, accompanied by his mutterings.

Then he tried on a second shirt, but again the button was missing. This shirt also went flying out the window, while Twain cursed more loudly.

He put on a third shirt, and when he found the

button was missing on this one, too, "I straightened up, gathered my reserves, and let myself go like a cavalry charge. In the midst of that great assault my eye fell upon that gaping door and I was paralyzed."

He stayed in the bathroom as long as possible, then crept into the bedroom, hoping against hope that Livy hadn't heard him. But when he looked at her, "I saw the gracious eyes with a something in them which I had never seen there before. They were snapping and flashing with indignation. I felt myself crumbling. . . . "

Livy, who had probably never sworn in her life, began repeating everything he had said.

"In my life time I had never heard anything so out of tune, so inharmonious, so incongruous, so ill suited to each other as were those mighty words set to that feeble music," Mark said. "I tried to keep from laughing, for I was a guilty person in deep need of charity and mercy. I tried to keep from bursting, and I succeeded — until she gravely said, 'There, now you know how it sounds.' "

In the spring of 1875, Twain found that his enthusiasm for *Tom Sawyer* had returned. He moved his study over the stable so he could have peace and quiet, and read the chapters to Livy as he finished them.

He copied the manuscript on a typewriter, a new invention he had first seen in a store window in Boston. The machine was still imperfect, however, and he quickly grew exasperated with it.

"Blame my cats," he wrote Howells, "but this thing requires genius in order to work it just right."

And on July 5, he wrote: "I have finished the story and didn't take the chap beyond boyhood. . . . If I went on now, and took him into manhood, he would just lie. . . . It is not a boy's book at all. It will only be read by adults. It is only written for adults.

"By & by I shall take a boy of twelve & run him on through life (in the first person) but not Tom Sawyer — he would not be a good character for it." This idea would grow into *The Adventures of Huckleberry Finn*.

Howells disagreed that *Tom Sawyer* was an adult book, and said it was "the best story I ever read. It will be an immense success, but I think you ought to treat it explicitly *as* a boy's story . . . if you should put it forth as a study of boy character from the grown-up point of view you give the wrong key to it."

Mark talked it over with Livy, then told Howells she "decides with you that the book should issue as a book for boys, pure & simple — & so do I."

Tom Sawyer was published in December 1876, and was largely ignored by critics. The only newspaper to review it was the *New York Times*, and the only literary journal to review it was Howells's *Atlantic Monthly*.

It was the immense success Howells had foreseen, however. Though some people complained that Tom and Huck were bad examples for children, most readers were fascinated by the story of their adventures in the Mississippi River town of St. Petersburg (St. Peter's place, or heaven).

Tom Sawyer lives with his Aunt Polly, a kind-

A sketch of Tom Sawyer, which appeared as the frontispiece in the 1879 edition of The Adventures of Tom Sawyer.

hearted widow who spends much of her time unsuccessfully trying to make him into the "Model Boy" of the village — an effort Tom isn't about to let succeed.

Near the beginning of the book, Tom has to whitewash a fence as punishment for skipping school. But, by pretending the job is fun, he manages to get other boys to do the work for him. Some even pay him for the privilege.

Throughout the book, Tom has one adventure after another: from stumbling across a murder when he and his friend, Huckleberry Finn, go to the graveyard one night, to getting lost in a huge cave with his girlfriend, Becky Thatcher. Tom spends much of his time trying to impress this "lovely little blue-eyed creature," who was modeled after a neighbor of Twain's named Laura Hawkins.

At the end of the book, Tom and Huck discover treasure in the cave and are admired by the townspeople for their newfound wealth. Huck, who had previously led a carefree life after being abandoned by his drunkard father, is adopted by the Widow Douglas.

Tom likes his new life, but Huck can't stand losing the freedom he once knew and decides to run away.

"The widder's good to me, and friendly; but I can't stand them ways," he tells Tom, when his friend finds him hiding in a big barrel. "She makes me git up just at the same time every morning; she makes me wash, they comb me all to thunder; she won't let me sleep in the wood-shed; I got to wear them blamed clothes that just smothers me . . .

"And dad fetch it, she prayed all the time! I never *see* such a woman! . . . And besides, that school's going to open, and I'd a had to go to it — well, I wouldn't stand *that*, Tom. Looky-here, Tom, being rich ain't what it's cracked up to be. . . . "

An illustration of Becky Thatcher.

But Huck finally agrees to go back to the Widow Douglas and "stick to the widder till I rot," in return for being allowed to join the robber gang Tom promises to organize.

Young people, especially, identified with this fantasy of boyhood where Work was defined as whatever a body was obliged to do, Play consisted of whatever a body was not obliged to do, and there were exciting places and emotions to explore.

Adults also loved the idyllic picture of boyhood that Twain painted. Long after Howells first read about Tom, Huck, and their friend Joe Harper hiding on an island in the river, he wrote: "I suppose we all have a Jackson's Island somewhere and dream of it when we are tired."

Interestingly, Twain almost totally ignored the black population in his idyllic town, but not quite. The main black character was the boy Jim, who was tricked by Tom into whitewashing the fence. Jim was loosely modeled after a child Mark had known as a youth and could never forget: Lewis, the young boy Twain's mother and father had owned.

Twain also had Huck discuss race prejudice and the hypocrisy that accompanies it, with a frankness that was unusual for the time.

"He likes me, becuz I don't ever act as if I was above him," Huck tells Tom of his friendship with the slave, Jake. "Sometimes I've set right down and eat *with* him. But you needn't tell that. A body's got to do things when he's awful hungry he wouldn't want to do as a steady thing."

But after writing *Tom Sawyer*, Twain again reverted to creating black stereotypes, as if someone else had written "A True Story" or penned Huck's insightful observations about racism.

During the two years following publication of *Tom Sawyer*, Twain wasted time writing two plays: *Ah Sin*, about a Chinese laundryman, and *Simon Wheeler, Detective*.

One critic said of *Ah Sin* that few plays "can be mentioned whose literary execution is so bad. . . . "

Twain then worked on his detective story, which included the most demeaning black character in all his writings.

No one would produce the play, however, and Twain decided it was "dreadfully witless and flat."

He had written the plays in the hope of making a lot of money in a hurry. The house at Hartford, with all Mark and Livy's socializing, was devouring money almost as fast as Mark could make it. They also had to pay for a staff that included Patrick McAleer, who cared for their horses and drove their carriage; Katy Leary, the housekeeper; and George Griffin, a "black and very handsome" man who was a combination butler, confidant of Mark, and playmate of the children.

"You see, I take a vile, mercenary view of things," Twain had written Howells about the best monetary arrangements for publishing *Tom Sawyer*, "but then my household expenses are something almost ghastly."

He realized he could not support his family as long as he took a "nine month vacation" at Hartford every year. He was also feeling worn down by the constant demands on his time.

"I have a badgered, harassed feeling a good part of my time," he told his mother. "It comes mainly of business responsibilities and annoyances, and the persecution of kindly letters from well meaning strangers."

He and Livy decided it would be cheaper to live in Europe, and that he would be able to write more there.

Twain also felt like leaving because of a speech he gave in honor of the poet, John Greenleaf Whittier, before New England's leading literary figures. Among those in the audience were poet Henry Wadsworth Longfellow, author Oliver Wendell Holmes, and poet and essayist Ralph Waldo Emerson.

In the speech, Twain pretended to be a miner whose cabin was invaded by three tramps calling themselves Longfellow, Holmes, and Emerson. The miner said the three proceeded to eat all his food, drink all his whiskey, and cheat at cards.

The audience was shocked, but Twain struggled along always hoping "that somebody would laugh, or that somebody would at least smile, but nobody did."

He finished the speech to a silence Howells described as "weighing many tons to the square inch," and Livy's distress was said to be so great "it is not to be measured."

"My sense of disgrace does not abate," Twain wrote Howells a few days later. He felt he had destroyed the friendships he had worked so hard to make.

He spent several months in Europe, working on a travel book to be called *A Tramp Abroad*. When he and Livy returned to the United States in September 1879, he continued to work on the book, but it was a struggle.

In July 1880, Livy gave birth to their fourth and last child, Jane Lampton Clemens. "Jean," as they called her, would be troubled with physical problems most of her life, but Livy said she was the healthiest-looking baby of all their children.

When Twain finally finished *A Tramp Abroad*, he began to work again on *The Prince and the Pauper*, his tale of a Prince (Edward VI) and a pauper who exchange places by accident.

Though Mark and Livy had gone abroad to save money, they began spending lavishly almost immediately on returning to Hartford.

There were large dinner parties, as well as many

smaller gatherings. In 1881, Twain spent over $100,000, including $40,000 on get-rich-quick schemes that returned almost nothing. His books were bringing in a lot of money, but he was spending it just as fast.

He confided to Howells that "a life of don't-care-a-damn in a boarding house is what I have asked for in many a secret prayer."

Clockwise, from far left: Clara, Livy, Jean, Mark, Susy— and Hash, the dog.

Twain had long fantasized about becoming rich from an invention — either his own or someone else's — just as he had once fantasized about finding gold lying on the ground.

Besides his self-pasting scrapbook, he invented adjustable straps for clothing and "Mark Twain's Memory-Builder," a game to teach history dates to children.

The scrapbook made money for 20 years, but most of it went to his partner. The only adjustable strap that was ever made was the one sent to the patent office, and by the time Twain completed the Memory-Builder — which he dreamed would bring him millions — the game was so complicated, few children in the world could have understood it.

He also poured money into other people's inventions, including a steam pulley, steam generator, cash register, marine telegraph, "plasmon" (a milk powder he swore would cure almost anything), and dozens of others.

He lost most of the money he invested, but with an almost infallible instinct for snatching economic defeat from the jaws of victory, he turned his back on the one invention that would have made him rich: the telephone.

When a young inventor named Alexander Graham Bell offered him stock in a device to carry the human voice over an electric wire, Twain declined.

"I said I didn't want anything more to do with wildcat speculation," he said.

Bell tried to persuade him to change his mind, and finally offered Twain all the stock he wanted for $500, but "I resisted all these temptations . . . went off with my check intact, and next day lent five thousand of it, on an unendorsed note, to a friend who was going to go bankrupt three days later."

One of Twain's favorite pastimes was playing billiards with friends in a special room on the third floor, and it was there a visitor told him of a machine that would change his life profoundly in the years ahead: the Paige Typesetter.

The Paige Typesetter, which was never completed, but drained Mark Twain's finances for 13 years.

Type was still being set by hand, as it was when Twain was a printer's apprentice. But now a man named James Paige, at the Colt Munitions Factory in Hartford, had invented a machine that would set type automatically. It was, he said, on the verge of being perfected.

Twain promised to invest $2,000, but promptly raised that to $5,000 once he saw the machine, convinced that enormous profits would soon start rolling in.

He also believed his finances would improve if he switched publishers, so he arranged for *The Prince and the Pauper* to be published by a friend, James R. Osgood, who had had no experience in subscription publishing. The result was that the book, in comparison with his previous ones, was a commercial failure.

The experience led Twain to begin making plans for his own publishing house, however, where he could control both production and profits.

Ever since writing the "Old Times on the Mississippi" articles for the *Atlantic* seven years before, he had wanted to revisit the scene of his youth. Now Osgood suggested he travel the length of the Mississippi and combine his fresh impressions with the articles to form a new subscription book, *Life on the Mississippi*.

The idea was for Twain to travel from St. Louis to New Orleans, then return upriver with Horace Bixby, the captain who taught him every bend and feature of the river. Osgood and a secretary would go with him.

Mark worried about Livy's reaction if he took a long trip, but she didn't mind. Though she knew she would miss him, she also knew his absence would mean relief from the constant pressure of entertaining visitors.

"This is my work," she said of her role as hostess, "and I know that I do very wrong when I feel chafed by it, but how can I be right about it? Sometimes it seems as if the simple sight of people would drive me *mad*. . . . I want so much to do other things to study and do things with the children and I cannot."

In the spring of 1882, Twain returned to the river of his youth and of his dreams.

His first sight of it in St. Louis was depressing, for the era of steamboating was almost over. At the wharf where he had once seen steamboats packed as tightly as sardines, he now saw only half a dozen deserted "lingering ghosts and remembrances of great fleets . . . "

But once under way on the steamboat *Gold Dust*, he recaptured the excitement of the past.

One morning he rose at four and went into the pilothouse, where he found it "fascinating to see the day steal gradually upon this vast silent world . . . "

There, he wrote Livy enthusiastically, he looked in awe at "the luxurious green walls of forest! & the jutting leafy capes! & the paling green of the far

stretches! & the remote, shadowy, vanishing dis-
tances, away down the glistening highway under the
horizon!"

Twain now seemed to think of himself as a Northerner, and criticized the way Southerners talked and
behaved, as if he had never heard them speak before
or shared their values. Most of all, he was disgusted
by the obsession of white Southerners with the Civil
War.

Everything that happened was dated as "befo' the
waw," "du'in the waw," or "right aftah the waw."

And in his notebook, Twain wrote: "People talk
only about the war. Other subjects are *started*, but
they soon pale & die & the war is taken up."

He said that white Southerners were obsessed by
the war because they still craved violence — the violence of the war and the violence of their slave society in the decades before the war.

Whereas the young Samuel Clemens had defended
slavery, the older Mark Twain felt that its abolition
was about the only improvement he could find in the
South.

Many white writers, especially Southerners, were
busy churning out "Wretched Freedman" stories that
glorified the pre–Civil War South. In their books,
they created a society where slaveowners were kind
and slaves were happy. They portrayed the ex-slaves,
by contrast, as miserable because they didn't know
what to do with their freedom and never wanted it.

One day Twain heard two black women talk about their experiences in slavery, with one telling the other how slaves were routinely killed on a nearby plantation and their bodies thrown in the river.

He promptly made a note to use the conversation in an article ridiculing stories about "the Wretched Freedman who longed for Slavery."

Twain stayed in New Orleans a few days before heading north with Bixby in his new steamboat, the *City of Baton Rouge*.

Bixby noticed that his former apprentice "was ever making notes in his memorandum-book, just as he always did."

Returning to Hannibal, Mark Twain spent three days visiting the scenes of his youth and "talking with the grey-heads who were boys and girls with me 30 or 40 years ago."

In his notebook he wrote, "Many of the people I once knew in Hannibal are now in heaven. Some, I trust, are in the other place."

He was tired now and anxious to leave a world that was so different from the one he remembered. Even the river had changed. It was in flood below St. Louis, and Twain saw buzzards fish for drowned men, and starving cattle strip the bark from trees.

The most profound change he discovered, however, was in the dreams of the young.

"The romance of boating is gone," he wrote. "In Hannibal the steamboatman is no longer a god. The

Tom Sawyer's house in Hannibal, Missouri, showing the famous fence from The Adventures of Tom Sawyer.

youth don't talk river slang any more. Their pride is apparently railroads. . . . "

It was time to go home.

Twain worked on the book all summer, but when fall came he still had 30,000 words to write and was thoroughly disgusted.

"I am going to write all day and two thirds of the

night, until the thing is done, or break down at it," he told Howells. "The spur and burden of the contract are intolerable to me. I can endure the irritation no longer."

He did 9,500 words in one day, "mainly stolen from books, tho' credit given," then decided not to write anymore until he felt like it.

To do otherwise, he declared, "would be to make the book worse than it already is."

He finally finished it at the end of 1882, calling it "this wretched . . . damned book."

Life on the Mississippi was really two books in one.

The *Atlantic* articles filled with his memories of his pre–Civil War years on the river comprised the first half of the book, while the second half was a description of his recent trip, with enough other material thrown in to fill out the book to its promised length.

In spite of Twain's negative feelings about the book, it was well received by critics and the public when it was published in the spring of 1883.

A typical comment appeared in the *Nation*, whose critic said the book was "only secondarily the work of a funny man," and was an important "descriptive and historical work."

The journey back to the Mississippi had renewed Twain's interest in the book about Huckleberry Finn he had begun seven years before. Old memories came flooding back to him, and his feelings about the South and the past now ran deeper and more powerfully than ever.

That summer at Quarry Farm he took out the half-finished manuscript and began to work on it again.

At first the work went slowly, but soon he was writing 3,000–4,000 words a day in his hilltop study.

"Why, it's like old times," he told Howells, "to step straight into the study, damp from the breakfast table, and sail right in and sail right on, the whole day long, without thought of running short of stuff or words. . . . And when I get fagged out, I lie abed a couple of days & read & smoke, & then go it again for 6 or 7 days."

Susy and Clara were now old enough to join Livy in commenting on the chapters as he finished them, and Mark enjoyed putting in outrageous passages he knew Livy would take out.

Near the end of August, Twain told Howells he had written eight or nine hundred pages and had nothing left to do but revise.

Most of the work on the manuscript that would become *The Adventures of Huckleberry Finn* was done. The story told of the shared adventures of a poor white youth and a black man seeking freedom, set in the slavery-time Missouri of Twain's childhood.

Its portrayal of everyday people and the dialects they spoke would earn Twain the reputation of father of the American novel. But on that long-ago summer day at Quarry Farm, it was enough for him that he had finally finished the story that so delighted him.

"And *I* shall *like* it," he wrote Howells, "whether anybody else does or not."

10

DEEP WATERS

The beginning of 1884 found Twain in a familiar situation, trying to figure out how to make more money.

He had used $56,000 of his own to publish *Life on the Mississippi*, and though the book sold fairly well, Twain was disappointed it didn't sell as well as his earlier books.

Having complete control of the publishing process had been a longtime dream, and now he decided to make the dream a reality by forming his own subscription publishing firm: Charles L. Webster and Company. Webster was his nephew-by-marriage, and had acted as his business manager the last three years.

Twain planned to publish *The Adventures of Huckleberry Finn* in time for Christmas, 1884, but told Webster "if we haven't forty thousand orders then, we simply postpone publishing till we've *got* them."

While Webster organized canvassers to solicit orders throughout the country, and supervised preparation of the book, Mark Twain went on a four-month lecture tour to earn more money.

Soon after the tour began, he heard that Ulysses S. Grant had decided to write his memoirs. Grant, hero of the Civil War and president for eight years, was penniless after investing in a fraudulent Wall Street brokerage house that had collapsed a few months earlier.

The Gilded Age that flourished under Grant had claimed him as one of its victims. He was now trying to pay his bills by writing Civil War articles for the *Century Magazine* at $500 an article (though Congress would soon pass a bill placing him on the retired army list with full pay).

Twain asked Grant to allow Webster & Company to publish his memoirs, and Grant agreed.

Mark resumed his tour, and soon discovered that he and Livy missed each other as keenly as when they were first engaged.

"I miss you, & I miss the children & would so unspeakably like to be with you," Twain wrote from Rochester, New York. " . . . I love you, sweetheart, that I know."

"Fifteen years married sixteen years engaged," Livy replied. "And . . . I love you with all my heart."

When Mark returned home for the Christmas holidays, Livy and the children surprised him with a stage performance of *The Prince and the Pauper*. A few days later they repeated the show for the entire neighborhood, and Twain played one of the roles.

"Papa acted his part beautifully . . . ," Susy wrote.

Clara and Susy in one of the Clemens family productions.

"He was inexpressibly funny, with his great slouch hat and gait — oh, such a gait! . . . He certainly could have been an actor as well as an author."

The proofs of *The Adventures of Huckleberry Finn* began coming from the printer in the spring, but they were too much for Twain to take.

"They don't make a very great many mistakes," he said of the printers, "but those that do occur are of a nature that make a man swear his teeth loose."

And in his notebook he wrote: "In the first place God made idiots. This was for practice. Then he made proofreaders."

Howells agreed to read the proofs for him, and the book was finally published in February 1885, after Webster's sales agents received orders for almost 40,000 copies.

Critics in the United States had been searching for "The Great American Novel" since the end of the Civil War. They urged authors to stop copying English and French writers, and to use American characters, settings, and themes instead. Mark Twain had done just that. Instead of praising him, though, most critics bitterly attacked him.

"If Mr. Clemens cannot think of something better to tell our pure-minded lads and lassies, he had better stop writing for them," declared Louisa May Alcott, author of *Little Women* and *Little Men*.

The Boston *Advertiser* editorialized that "Mark Twain has shown talents and industry which, now that his last effort has failed so ignominiously, we trust he will employ in some manner more creditable to himself and more beneficial to the country."

And the Public Library Committee of Concord, Massachusetts, banned the book, denouncing it as "trash and suitable only for the slums."

In *Huckleberry Finn*, Mark made heroes of two outcasts: the rowdy Huck and the runaway slave, Jim, and denounced Southern society's widespread acceptance of violence, ignorance, and bigotry.

He attacked church, state, school, and parents for teaching that comforting, feeding, or helping a runaway slave was "a low-down thing" God would punish "with everlasting fire."

In writing the book, Mark Twain reached back into his childhood memories, including a time when his father took an elderly slave named Charley on a "hard and tedious journey" in midwinter, and then sold him as cold-heartedly as if "this humble comrade of his long pilgrimage had been an ox — & somebody else's ox."

The price his father received for Charley in real life was the price Twain gave the men who betrayed Jim in the book: forty dollars.

The first words in *Huckleberry Finn* are: "You don't know about me, without you have read a book by the name of 'The Adventures of Tom Sawyer' . . . "

The words are spoken by Huck, the narrator of the story. The money he found in *Tom Sawyer* has brought him nothing but trouble, and in order to escape from his father — who kidnaps and beats him in his efforts to steal the money — Huck fakes his own murder and flees to Jackson's Island.

There he discovers Jim, who ran away because he was afraid he was about to be sold "down the river" where slaves were treated much more brutally than in St. Petersburg. (Jim is routinely called "Nigger Jim" by teachers and critics, but Twain refers to him throughout the book as "Jim.") The person talking about selling him is Tom Sawyer's aunt and guardian, the pious but slave-owning Aunt Polly. Huck

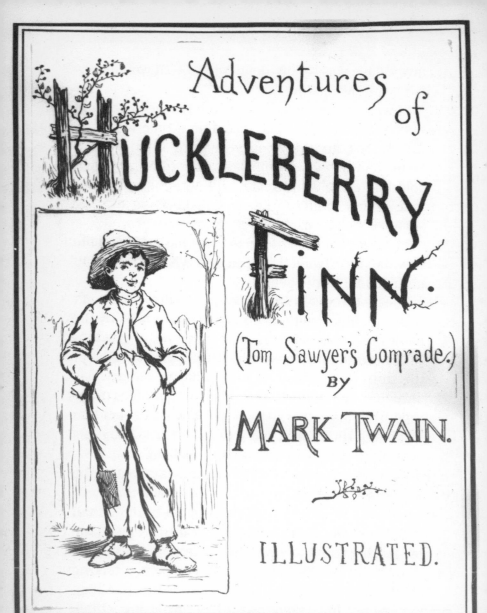

The cover drawing for the first edition of
Huckleberry Finn.

promises not to betray Jim, even though people "would call me a low down Abolitionist and despise me for keeping mum . . . "

Huck and Jim — one young, one old; one white, one black — become fellow seekers after freedom, and protectors of each other as they float down the Mississippi on a raft. And on that raft, they manage to create a community of brotherhood far different from the divisive life they have known on land.

"What you want, above all things, on a raft, is for everybody to be satisfied, and feel right and kind towards the others," Huck explains.

But the raft cannot keep the real world of the shore from intruding on their lives, and they are forced to deal with the slavery, murder, lynching, feuds, and hypocrisy of "civilized" society.

Once Huck attends a church service where two feuding families heartily approve of the sermon they hear about brotherly love "and such-like tiresomeness," in the words of Huck. But the next day they renew their feud and savagely kill each other, even though no one can remember why the feud began decades before.

"It made me so sick . . . ," Huck said. "I ain't agoing to tell all that happened . . . I wished I hadn't ever come ashore that night to see such things. I ain't ever going to get shut of them — lots of times I dream about them."

Throughout the book, Twain showed the appalling

difference between the good things people say they believe in and the horrible deeds they do.

This is the "civilization" that Huck and Jim are both fleeing. Huck's struggle to discover and do what is right is shown most powerfully in the famous "Conscience" scene, where the values he was taught by adults make him believe that right is wrong and wrong is right.

His conscience forces him to write a letter to the woman who owned Jim, Miss Watson, telling where she could find him.

"I felt good and washed clean of sin for the first time I had ever felt so in my life, and I knowed I could pray now," said Huck. "But I didn't do it straight off, but laid the paper down and set there thinking . . . and I see Jim before me, all the time, in the day, and in the night-time, sometimes moonlight, sometimes storms, and we a floating along, talking, and singing, and laughing. But somehow I couldn't seem to strike no places to harden me against him, but only the other kind. I'd see him standing my watch on top of his'n . . . and at last I struck the time I saved him by telling the men we had small-pox aboard, and he was so grateful, and said I was the best friend old Jim ever had in the world, and the *only* one he's got now; and then I happened to look around, and see that paper.

"It was a close place. I took it up, and held it in my hand. I was a trembling, because I'd got to decide, forever, betwixt two things, and I knowed it. I studied a minute, sort of holding my breath, and then says to myself:

"'All right, then I'll go to hell' — and tore it up.

"It was awful thoughts, and awful words, but they was said. And I let them stay said, and never thought no more about reforming."

Though few critics specifically denounced Mark Twain's portrayal of society's twisted values, or his attack on the whole concept that black people were subhuman, he was certain most of their criticism came because of those portrayals.

The fathers of those same critics, he charged angrily, had "shouted the same blasphemies a genera-

An illustration of Huckleberry Finn, from the 1885 edition of the book.

tion earlier when they were closing their doors against the hunted slave."

The book quickly sold over 50,000 copies. It was also popular in England, where many recognized it as a masterpiece and the London *Saturday Review* said some passages had "poetry and pathos blended in their humor. . . . In Mark Twain, the world has a humorist who is yearly ripening and mellowing."

In the months following publication of *Huckleberry Finn*, Twain devoted much of his time to overseeing the preparation of Grant's book. Grant discovered he was suffering from cancer, and didn't think he could write, but Twain supplied him with a stenographer. The old general was then able to dictate as much as 10,000 words a day.

In the meantime, Twain and Charles Webster were busy ordering vast quantities of paper, contracting with printers, and organizing an army of sales agents. By the first of May, orders had poured in for 60,000 sets of the two-volume *Memoirs*.

Near the end of July, Grant scrawled some last-minute changes on paper, then "put his pencil aside, and said he was done — there was nothing more to do." Three days later, he was dead.

His *Memoirs* were published a few weeks after his death, and the public's response was overwhelming. One hundred thousand sets of the two volumes had been ordered even before he finished writing them, and another 200,000 were sold in the months that followed. His widow earned over $400,000 from the books.

Years later, Twain said it would have been better if he had been struck dead the moment he decided to publish Grant's book, but his immediate reaction was one of joy and disbelief.

"I am frightened at the proportions of my prosperity," he told a friend one night. "It seems to me that whatever I touch turns to gold."

He used some of his money to help others, including several black students. In 1882, Twain had given $2,500 for scholarships to all-black Lincoln University in Lincoln, Pennsylvania, and paid for the Paris apprenticeship of Charles Ethan Porter, a black artist.

Now he paid the expenses of several other black students, including Warner Thornton McGuinn, one of the first members of his race to graduate from Yale Law School. Twain met McGuinn when the latter introduced him as a speaker at the university, and was very impressed by him. (Later, McGuinn worked briefly with Thurgood Marshall, who went on to become the first black justice of the United States Supreme Court.)

Throughout this time, Twain continued to invest heavily in Paige's typesetter, which he was still convinced would bring him millions. But Paige was never satisfied with his invention, and kept asking for money to make some "final" improvement.

Twain's friend and financial advisor, F.G. Whitmore, warned that the project would bankrupt him if he kept pouring money into it, but Twain wouldn't listen.

His other fantasy of wealth revolved around the publishing firm. The huge successes of *Huckleberry Finn* and Grant's *Memoirs* blinded him and Webster to the fact that neither really knew how to run a publishing business.

Twain quickly contracted for several more books, including accounts of their Civil War experiences by Generals William Sherman, Philip Sheridan, and Samuel Crawford. His biggest project of all was to be *The Life of Pope Leo XIII*.

"He had no words in which to paint the magnificence of the project or to forecast its colossal success," Howells said. "It would have a currency bounded only by the number of Catholics in Christendom. It would be translated into every language which was anywhere written or printed; it would be circulated literally in every country of the globe."

Webster traveled to Rome and met the pope, who gave his sanction and blessing to the book. So much of Twain's time was now taken up by business matters, he had little time for writing.

Susy, who had started writing a biography of her father, said in it that "Mama and I have been very much troubled of late because papa, since he had been publishing General Grant's books, has seemed to forget his own books and works entirely; and the other evening, as papa and I were promonading [sic] up and down the library, he told me that he didn't expect to write but one more book, and then he was ready to give up work altogether, die, or do anything. . . . "

Twain occasionally worked on the book that would become *A Connecticut Yankee in King Arthur's Court*, but told Mrs. Fairbanks he expected to take thirty years to finish it. He now seemed more interested in being so rich he didn't have to write, than in continuing to write.

A Connecticut Yankee, he told Howells, "is my swan-song, my retirement from literature permanently . . . "

In the summer of 1886, the family traveled to Keokuk to visit his mother, who was living with Orion.

Part of the trip was by steamboat. The first evening, Twain stood by himself listening to the leadsman's calls as he sounded the river's depths. Finally, as the leadsman measured two fathoms, he called out: "Mark Twain, Mark Twain."

Suddenly Clara came running down the deck.

"Papa," she said breathlessly, "I have hunted all over the boat for you. Don't you know they are calling for you?"

The months to come proved increasingly disappointing for Mark Twain, the publisher. None of the books that came after Grant's *Memoirs* made much money. Even *The Life of Pope Leo XIII*, published simultaneously in six languages and expected to make millions, barely showed a profit.

The disappointing sales, combined with Twain's expenditure of several thousand dollars a month on Paige's typesetter and tens of thousands a year to run the household, began to revive Twain's old fears of financial ruin.

For Christmas, 1887, he sent his sister Pamela $15. "If we weren't a little crowded this year by the type-setter I'd send a check large enough to buy a family Bible or some other useful thing like that," he wrote. "However, we go on & on, but the type-setter goes on forever — at $3,000 a month. . . . We'll be through now in 3 or 4 months, I reckon, & then the strain will let up. . . . "

But the strain didn't let up.

The firm, which had been greatly expanded in order to publish Grant's book, required large amounts of money to break even. Adding to Twain's troubles was a bookkeeper's embezzlement of $30,000. His biggest problem of all, however, was Charles Webster.

The firm had been structured so Webster could have final decision-making authority over its operations. Twain said he accepted "several excellent books but Webster declined them every time, and he was the master. But if anybody offered *him* a book, he was so charmed with the compliment that he took the book without examining it." Most of the books Webster accepted were financial failures.

Twain was now becoming desperate about the financial condition of the firm, and wrote in his notebook: "Demand a reconstruction of the contract placing power in my hands where it belongs. . . . Can I be held for debts made beyond the captial? I will buy or sell out.

"Since the spring of 1886, the thing has gone straight down hill, towards sure destruction. It must be brought to an end, February 1 [1888], at all hazards. This is final."

In the midst of his troubles Twain managed to find time to complete *A Connecticut Yankee in King Arthur's Court*, though he complained that Webster "published it so surreptitiously that it took two or three years to find out that there was any such book."

A Connecticut Yankee told about a foreman in an arms factory in Hartford, who was knocked unconscious and woke up in the England of King Arthur's day.

Twain used the book to again express his loathing of anyone in authority (medieval kings, in this case), who used their power to oppress people.

He enlarged on this theme in the book, having

King Arthur captured and sold as a slave while he wandered in disguise in his realm.

"The blunting effects of slavery upon the slaveholder's moral perceptions are known and conceded the world over," his Yankee foreman says, "and a privileged class, an aristocracy, is but a band of slaveholders under another name."

A Connecticut Yankee delighted American readers, but was ignored or attacked by most English critics. In the years to come, when Twain criticized loyalty and patriotism as practiced by his fellow Americans, much of their delight would also turn to anger.

A Connecticut Yankee was published in 1889, but did little to halt Twain's slide toward financial ruin. His money was almost gone, and he tried to sell stock to pay the master mechanics still struggling to make the latest "final" adjustments on Paige's typesetter. But no one was interested.

He was offered a 50 percent share in the rival Mergenthaler linotype, which was said to be almost complete, in exchange for giving its developers a 50 percent interest in the Paige. But Twain, as optimistic as ever about Paige's invention, refused the offer. A few years later, the Mergenthaler stock was worth millions.

"The Paige Compositor marches alone and far in the land of human inventions," Twain declared.

In 1890, he paid out $4,000 a month on the "cunning devil," a sum that was swallowing his income and Livy's inheritance.

He wrote a note to Paige, saying he would not spend any more money on the machine. But he went on spending anyway, as if he were somehow powerless to stop himself. Twain was now wasting years in a vain pursuit of wealth for his family. His and Livy's happiest years were over.

He vented his anger in long letters and in monologues to his family about the shortcomings of mankind in general, and the specific man or woman he was angry with that day. Though Twain didn't know it, his daughters were afraid of his anger.

Once, after Twain wrote a furious letter about a woman who had been a guest in their house, Livy said in desperation: "Youth darling . . . I am absolutely wretched to-day on account of your state of mind . . . change your mental attitude, *try to change it*. The trouble is you don't want to. . . . Does it help the world to always rail at it? . . . "

In the fall of 1890, the mothers of Livy and Mark both passed away. They grieved together for the loved ones they had lost, and for the shared dreams that were now slipping away.

Adding to Twain's depression was the fact that eighteen-year-old Susy, his favorite child, had left for her freshman year at Bryn Mawr College in Pennsylvania. He missed the comradeship they had en-

Susy (left) and Clara Clemens in 1890.

joyed, and the intimate conversations where they
shared their hopes and dreams.

He visited her so often, said one classmate, that
Livy "would come down occasionally for a short
stay, I think in order to keep Mr. Clemens from coming, because she told me that he would make any-

thing an excuse, even to bringing down Olivia's laundry."

By the beginning of 1891, Twain had sunk $190,000 into the typesetter, with no end in sight. The publishing business was kept afloat only by the money he pumped into it. He cashed every security the family owned, and signed notes to keep the business going.

Royalties from his books could not even cover household expenses, and the publishing and invention costs were steadily rising. He and Livy searched desperately for a way out, and their answer was the same one they had come up with in 1878: Move to Europe, where living costs were cheaper.

On a warm day in June 1891, they closed the house in Hartford. Livy was the last to leave their home of 17 years, moving slowly from room to room, before finally closing the front door behind her.

She was 46 years old, and would never see the house again.

They sailed for Europe, not knowing they would spend most of the next decade there. For the first time in 20 years, Twain found himself totally dependent on his writing for his income.

He worked as hard as he could, turning out several magazine and newspaper articles, even though rheumatism often bothered him so much he could barely use his right arm.

He started to write a "howling farce" for *Century*

magazine about the adventures of Siamese twins, but changed his mind partway through and sent off a drastically different story.

"It'll furnish me cash for awhile, I reckon," he said.

The story would become his novel *The Tragedy of Pudd'nhead Wilson*, and was built around an issue that had fascinated him most of his life and caused so much trouble in Nevada: miscegenation.

Southern white critics were furious at Twain's challenging their racial beliefs and practices, which, at the time he wrote *Pudd'nhead*, included widespread lynchings and the violent denial of the right of black men to vote.

One Southern critic said the book should have been called "The Decline and Fall of Mark Twain."

Twain continued to concentrate on his writing, but often walked the floor at night, disturbed by both business worries and pain from rheumatism that sometimes made it hard for him to hold a pen. Several times, he interrupted his work for frantic trips to the United States to try and save his crumbling enterprises, but they were past saving. "The billows of hell have been rolling over me," he wrote Livy during one trip.

By the time Webster & Company finally declared bankruptcy in the spring of 1894, Twain had lost $110,000 of his money and $60,000 of Livy's. He also owed $100,000 to the firm's creditors, who demanded the house in Hartford and the copyrights to all his books (copyrights Twain was willing to give up because he thought they would soon be worthless).

Henry Rogers, an executive from Standard Oil who had befriended him, negotiated with the creditors and managed to save both the house and copyrights.

After years of worrying about Webster & Company, the bankruptcy was actually a relief to Twain, and for a while he wrote with an enthusiasm he hadn't felt for years. He was also still hopeful that Paige would perfect the typesetter, though those hopes were rapidly dwindling.

In his notebook he described Paige as a man who "could persuade a fish to come out and take a walk with him." Twain had been the fish for thirteen years, and now he was disillusioned and angry.

The end came in December 1894, when Rogers wrote a letter saying it was hopeless to sink any more money into the typesetter. Twain was expecting the news but still, he wrote Rogers, "It hit me like a thunderclap. It knocked every rag of sense out of my head, and I went flying here and there and yonder, not knowing what I was doing."

Livy spent hours trying to calm him, and finally succeeded.

"Nothing daunts Mrs. Clemens or makes the world

look black to her," Twain told Rogers, "which is the reason I haven't drowned myself."

He was childlike in his gratefulness to the man who worked tirelessly to try and straighten out his tangled financial affairs.

"I am 59 years old," Twain wrote him, "yet I never had a friend before who put out a hand and tried to pull me ashore when he found me in deep waters."

Twain now had more time for his writing, and soon finished *Personal Recollections of Joan of Arc*, a subject that had haunted him since that day in Hannibal when he picked up the windblown page that told about her sufferings.

In February, he made a quick business trip to the United States, then returned to Europe and brought his family back to the United States.

Though he hated lecturing as much as ever, Twain wrote Mrs. Fairbanks that he would "have to mount the platform next fall or starve."

He was also determined to pay his creditors every cent they had lost, even though he wasn't legally obligated to do so.

"But I am not a businessman," he said to reporters, "and honor is a harder master than the law. It cannot compromise for less than 100 cents on the dollar. . . ."

Twain decided on a world tour, which would also give him material for another travel book. The tour and the book combined, he hoped, would allow him to pay off all his debts in four years.

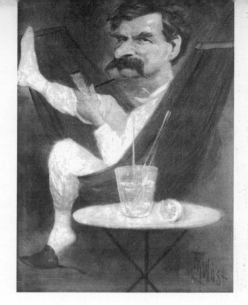

A humorous oil painting of Mark Twain.

The family went to Quarry Farm for several weeks, the first visit they had made in years. Twain was unable to walk because of a huge carbuncle on his foot, but finally was well enough to leave. Jean was too young for the trip, and the frail Susy — who had begun studying to be an opera singer — decided to follow her teacher's advice "to live on a hill . . . and gather vigor of body."

On July 14, 1895, with Susy crying and blowing kisses from the platform, they left Elmira by train for a 19-city tour of the northern United States.

One of Twain's lectures was in Butte, Montana, where he was a guest at a performance of the all-black 10th U.S. Cavalry regimental band. He was also escorted throughout the day by one of the "Buffalo Soldiers," as Native Americans called the black cavalrymen.

"Splendid big negro soldiers," Twain wrote in his notebook. ". . . They all have the look and bearing of gentlemen. . . . *I* think the negro has found his vocation at last."

In August, Twain and his family sailed from Vancouver, British Columbia, on a journey that would take them to Australia, New Zealand, Ceylon, India, South Africa, and England.

"We lectured and robbed and raided for thirteen months," he said. "I sent the lecture money to Mr. Rogers as fast as we captured it."

The tour was hard on him, and he was often ill or discouraged. But packed houses greeted him everywhere, and he loved the hours spent on stage.

"The doctor says I am on the verge of being a sick man," he told one audience in Melbourne, Australia, "[but] I don't take any stock in that. I have been on the verge of being an angel all my life, but it's never happened yet."

A year to the day they left Elmira, they sailed from South Africa for England, where they expected Susy and Jean to join them.

Mark felt more optimistic than he had in years, but word soon came that Susy was ill with spinal meningitis. A few days later, after Livy and Clara had sailed for the United States to be with her, Mark wrote he "was standing in our dining-room, thinking of nothing in particular," when a cablegram was handed to him that read: " 'Susy was peacefully released to-day.' "

The family happiness that was his fondest dream was gone forever.

11

NIGHT OF DEATH

It was as if the years rolled away, and he was confronted once again with the "dumb sense of vast loss" he had known with the death of his brother, Henry, and his son, Langdon.

During the days following Susy's death, in moods alternating from grief to rage, he waited in vain for a letter from his relatives or friends. But the only word of sympathy he received came from his publisher, Harper & Brothers.

". . . I sit back & try to believe that there are any human beings in the world, friends or foes, civilized or savage, who would close their lips there, & leave me these many, many, many days eating my heart out with longings for the tidings that never come," he wrote Livy eight days after Susy's death. "I think that Jean could have remembered me . . . or Twichell, or somebody."

As he had in the deaths of Henry and Langdon, he blamed himself for Susy's death. ". . . my crimes made her a pauper and an exile," he wrote Livy in despair.

He remembered how he had waved good-bye to

Susy as they left Elmira for the trip around the world, knowing she was "unhappy to be left alone." But he had gone, he said bitterly, for the sake "of honor — honor — honor — no rest, comfort, joy — but plenty of honor, plenty of ethical glory."

And in return for his determination to be honorable, he lost the child who was closest to him — the child who was like a young, feminine version of himself.

"She was a poet," he wrote in his notebook, "a poet whose song died unsung."

Twain wrote Twichell that while he had known "Susy was part of us . . . I did *not* know that she could go away, and take our lives with her; yet leave our dull bodies behind."

He chastised himself because, although he had often felt like saying, " 'You marvelous child!' . . . [I] never said it. To my sorrow I remember it now."

But most of all, he blamed himself for being far away while she wandered in delirium through the house, calling for her mother. He blamed himself for being far away while spinal meningitis, with its "night of death [was] closing around her . . . "

Livy, Clara, and Jean arrived in Elmira for the funeral on the same train and in the same car that had taken Livy, Clara, and Mark on their westward journey one year, one month, and one week before.

Mother and daughters followed the hearse with

Susy in it to the family plot in Elmira, where they laid her to rest beside Langdon — "she that had been our wonder and our worship."

Then they joined Twain in a rented house in London, where the four lived like hermits for the next several months while they tried to heal. Adding to the family's worries was the discovery that Jean suffered from epilepsy, and had begun to have daily seizures — sometimes more than a dozen a day.

Twain was seen in public so rarely that rumors circulated he was sick and poverty-stricken, and had been deserted by his family.

A reporter was sent to check on a rumor he was dead, and Twain told him: "Just say the report of my death has been grossly exaggerated."

Often he picked up the biography Susy had begun so many years before, and read again the first line she had written: "We are a very happy family."

He sought solace in his writing and, to his amazement, found it. "I couldn't get along without work now," he told Howells, describing how he often wrote eight or nine hours a day, seven days a week.

He worked on his book about the round-the-world trip throughout the winter, and finished it in May 1897. *Following the Equator* would be the last of his travel books and the angriest.

The book also contained some of the most powerful denunciations of oppression ever written.

Throughout Asia and Africa, Twain had seen how European democracies — with the blessing of the church — used brute force to enslave and destroy dark-skinned people and steal their land.

Almost alone among the American writers of his time, he scorned the excuses they gave for doing this: the "white man's burden" argument that Europeans were bringing "civilization" to Asia and Africa.

"There are many humorous things in the world," Twain wrote, "among them the white man's notion that he is less savage than other savages."

And then he listed all kinds of atrocities committed by white people in one land after another.

"In more than one country we have hunted the savage and his little children and their mother with dogs and guns through the woods and swamps, for an afternoon's sport, and filled the region with happy laughter over their sprawling and stumbling flight, and their wild supplications for mercy. . . . We have taken the savage's land from him, and made him our slave. . . . "

A critic in the magazine the *Chap Book* said Twain had become "ethical-minded and solemn," and "there is no hope for him."

Most critics seemed to agree, but that didn't stop him. For the remaining thirteen years of his life, he would use the power of his pen to denounce injustice wherever he found it.

Mark Twain's famous friend, Helen Keller.

Helen Keller, the famous blind and deaf young woman Twain befriended at this time, said later: "He thought he was a cynic, but his cynicism did not make him indifferent.... He would often say, 'Helen, the world is full of staring, soulless eyes.' He would work himself into a frenzy over dull acquiescence in any evil that could be remedied."

In the summer, Twain moved his family to a small village near Lucerne, Switzerland. While Livy and his daughters relaxed or went sightseeing, he worked on four or five books, but eventually abandoned them all.

He was beginning to enjoy life again, though, surrounded by the "superb scenery whose beauty undergoes a perpetual change from one miracle to another . . . "

Twain had been awestruck when he heard the Fisk Jubilee Singers in London in 1873. All of them were young ex-slaves, and they sang to raise money to start a black school: Fisk University in Nashville, Tennessee.

They were usually not allowed to sleep or eat in hotels in the United States, but were treated like royalty in Europe.

On a warm evening in August, Mark and Livy entered the village beer hall where the singers were about to perform.

Inside was "a crowd of German and Swiss men and women . . . ," Twain wrote Twichell, "with their beer mugs in front of them — self-contained and unimpressionable looking people. . . . The Singers got up and stood — the talking and glass jingling went on. Then rose and swelled out above those common earthly sounds one of those rich chords the secret of whose make only the Jubilees possess, and a spell fell upon that house. . . . Away back in the beginning — to my mind — their music made all other vocal music cheap; and that early notion is emphasized now. It is utterly beautiful, to me; and it moves me infinitely more than any other music can."

He and Livy invited the singers to their house, and

the next day Mark wrote in his notebook: "They are as fine people as I am acquainted with in any country."

In the fall, he moved the family to Vienna so Clara could study piano with a renowned teacher, and a few weeks later they received word that Orion had died. The brother Twain described as having "three hundred and sixty five red-hot new eagernesses every year" of his life, died a poor man at the age of seventy-two "with a pen in his hand . . . jotting down the conflagration for that day . . . "

Twain spent much of his time in Vienna writing tales, sketches, and essays that would go into his next book, *The Man That Corrupted Hadleyburg and Other Stories*.

Though the title story was a searing condemnation of man's hypocrisy and weakness, Twain told Howells "the first half of the story — and I hope three-fourths — will be comedy. . . . I think I can carry the reader a long way before he suspects that I am laying a tragedy-trap."

He was writing just seven years before a teenager named Adolf Hitler would come to Vienna and start building a political career based on lies, and one of the essays in the book was an eerily prophetic warning of the danger of "the lie of silent assertion."

The blueprints for the lie of silent assertion and the barbarities that inevitably followed, he declared, had been drawn in the United States decades before.

"For instance: It would not be possible for a humane and intelligent person to invent a rational excuse for slavery," he wrote, "yet you will remember that in the early days of the emancipation agitation in the North, the agitators got but small help or countenance from any one. Argue and plead and pray as they might, they could not break the universal stillness that reigned, from pulpit and press all the way down to the bottom of society — the clammy stillness created and maintained by the lie of silent assertion — the silent assertion that there wasn't anything going on in which humane and intelligent people were interested."

It was also in Vienna that Twain received the news he had waited so long to hear: all his creditors had finally been paid, and there was money to spare.

Less than a month after escaping from his nightmare of debt, however, he was eagerly negotiating for the American rights to a carpet-making machine he said would make him millions.

In the summer of 1899, Mark took Jean to a sanitarium in Sweden in hopes of finding a cure for her. She seemed to improve, and a few months later the family moved to London so she could continue the treatments.

"I am tired of this everlasting exile," Twain wrote Rogers a few weeks later. It had been nine years since Mark and Livy left to live in Europe, and they decided it was finally time to go home.

They arrived in New York City on October 15, 1900, and Twain told a reporter who came on board the ship: "If I ever get ashore I am going to break both of my legs so I can't get away again."

Newspapers throughout the country ran editorials welcoming him home, and throngs greeted him wherever he went.

Livy and Mark Twain.

"One could never begin to describe in words the atmosphere of adulation that swept across his threshold," Clara remembered years later. "Every day was like some great festive occasion."

Unable to face returning to the house in Hartford now that Susy was dead, Twain and the family settled in New York City (they sold the house a few months later). Reporters asked his opinion about every subject under the sun, and he was more than happy to give it.

His first evening home, he criticized the country's military policy in the Philippine Islands, saying: "I . . . have seen that we do not intend to free but to subjugate the people of the Philippines. We have gone there to conquer, not to redeem."

Howells had become a leader in the country's rapidly growing anti-imperialist movement, which not only denounced U.S. policy in the Philippines, but the colonialist policies of Great Britain and other countries in Africa and China.

In his tour around the world, Twain had seen the Western nations' scramble for markets and resources in other peoples' lands, and the exploitation that went with it. That exploitation reminded Twain of the slavery he had known in Hannibal, so he readily agreed when Howells asked him to become a spokesperson for the anti-imperialist movement.

The nation that had been virtually unanimous in welcoming him home was now bitterly divided about whether he was welcome or not.

Twain "drew thunder and lightning about him," said Clara. ". . . Cutting, abusive letters and newspaper attacks flooded our home . . . and it was pathetic to see the effect they had on Mother. She was sure that they must cause her husband pain, however valiantly he might conceal it, and this was hard for her to endure."

Far from showing signs of pain, however, Twain lost himself in a happy frenzy of speech-making, entertaining, and writings that both pleased and infuriated the public.

The new year had hardly begun when the *North American Review* published his "To the Person Sitting in Darkness," a brilliantly satirical denunciation of the missionary movement as a tool of Western imperialism in China and other countries.

Before publishing the article, he showed it to Livy and Howells, and received their approval. Their opinions alone, Clara said, "could enable him to stand like the Statue of Liberty, unweakened by the waters of condemnation that washed up to his feet."

Twichell warned him that publication would hurt his book sales, and Twain said Howells advised him to "go hang myself first, and when I asked him what I should do that for, he said to save the public the trouble, because when that story appeared in print they would surely hang me."

Twain attacked missionaries who collected huge amounts of money and property for the deaths of Christians during the Boxer Rebellion: a Chinese revolt against the Europeans, Americans, and Japanese who occupied part of their land.

But he saved his most bitter criticism for the U.S. government's killing of Filipinos fighting for their freedom, saying: "What we wanted . . . was the Archipelago unencumbered by patriots struggling for independence; and War was what we needed."

The article was the bugle call anti-imperialists had been waiting for, but it infuriated other Americans. Some said he was a writer of humor who had no business discussing serious matters, while others called him a traitor.

But Twain seemed unbothered by the criticism, and soon wrote an article connecting conquest abroad and oppression of black Americans at home.

In "The United States of Lyncherdom," he asked readers to imagine what it would have looked like if the 203 black men, women, and children lynched in the United States in 1900, had all been killed at the same time and place.

There would be "twenty-four miles of blood-and-flesh bonfires unbroken," with "no sound but the soft moaning of the wind and the muffled sobbing of the sacrifices."

He planned to publish the article in the *North American Review* in the fall, and also use it as the introduction to a book he planned to write "to be called 'History of Lynching in America' — or some such title. . . . "

His publisher warned him that if he printed such a book, he would not have "even half a friend left" in the South. Twain must have known this even before he wrote the article.

But whether for fear of offending white Southerners, which seems unlikely given his other harsh writings about them and his continued determination to write the book, or because he eventually lost interest in the project as he did so many others, "The United States of Lyncherdom" was not published during his lifetime.

Later in the year, however, he urged passage of a federal law to at least prohibit white Southerners from lynching black people on Christmas Day (no U.S. president in Twain's lifetime supported a federal law to punish lynchings).

Twain also became active in the movement to gain women the right to vote. Years before he had ridiculed the women's rights movement, but now he gave speeches supporting it.

"I don't care who makes the laws," he declared, "so long as I can see the whip lash of the ballot in woman's hand. . . . "

His friendship with Isabella Beecher Hooker probably had much to do with his change of heart, just as his relationship with Livy and her family helped change his views about black people.

But in both cases, he had often felt uneasy about his prejudices even while he was defending them. When a woman attacked his criticism of the women's rights cause in 1867, for instance, his reply was weak and halfhearted.

The answer would have been much better, he confided to a friend, "if she hadn't all the arguments on her side."

Years later, he praised Isabella Hooker and other women's rights leaders for their struggle which "lasted a great many years, and is the most wonderful in history, for it achieved a revolution — the only one achieved in history for the emancipation of a nation that cost not a drop of blood. They broke the chains of their sex and set it free."

The hectic social life of Twain and his family continued without letup, and they were glad to spend a quiet summer at Saranac Lake in the Adirondacks.

In the fall they moved to a house just outside New York City, where Livy's heart bothered her so much, that she was confined to bed throughout the winter. The doctor did not allow Twain to see her, and they communicated by writing notes.

"Good morning, sweetheart," he said in one, "it is bright and beautiful and I love you most deeply. . . . I wish you were down here sweetheart."

And in one of her replies, Livy wrote: "Youth my own precious Darling . . .

"I miss you sadly, sadly. Your note in the morning gave me support for the day, the one at night, peace for the night. With the deepest love of my heart,

"Your Livy."

Twain told Clara "in his funny little self-accusing way, 'I wouldn't go in to see your mother, even if the doctor permitted it, for I would surely give out some startling yarn that would make the hair of a wolf stand on end.' "

He missed Livy's help on practical matters, including resolving a question she had raised about their lease on the house.

"My understanding was — was — was — oh, well dang it I don't know what it was — I don't reckon I had any," he wrote her about his agreement with the owner. "Often I have an understanding that I don't understand, and then I come to find out I didn't."

Livy's health gradually improved, and Mark was able to concentrate more on his writing.

In June 1902, Twain traveled to Columbia, Missouri, to receive an honorary Doctor of Laws degree from the University of Missouri.

"If I am not called at least 'Doc' from now on," he said, "there will be a decided coolness."

Twain prided himself on his lack of formal education, but was tremendously pleased when his accomplishments were recognized by leaders in colleges and universities.

Several days before the ceremonies, he took a

train for Hannibal and what he knew would be his last visit to his childhood home. He spoke at the high school graduation, and also at the church, where there was so much applause, he wrote Livy, "I had to stand silent a long minute till I could speak without my voice breaking."

As he stood on the train platform waiting to leave,

Mark Twain in front of his boyhood home in Hannibal, Missouri.

" MARK TWAIN AND HIS BOYHOOD HOME " HANNIBAL-MO. ©PHOTO BY-H.TOMLINSON.
1902 COPY PHOTO BY JERN AND HAL FRAZER
FRAZER STUDIO, HANNIBAL, MO

a man approached and Twain instantly recognized him. It was Tom Nash, a friend who almost drowned one night when the river ice broke while they were out skating. Nash had been deaf ever since.

"He was old and white-headed, but the boy of 15 was still visible in him," Twain said. "He came up to me, made a trumpet of his hands at my ear, nodded his head towards the citizens and said confidentially — in a yell like a fog horn — 'same damned fools, Sam!' "

When Twain returned home, he and Livy rented a cottage for the summer in York Harbor, Maine. It promised to be a happy time and was for a while, but on August 12, Livy was stricken with what seemed to be a violent heart attack.

"She could not breathe — was likely to stifle," Twain wrote in his notebook. "Also she had severe palpitation. She believed she was dying. I also believed it."

A doctor said she was suffering from heart disease and nervous prostration, and he ordered that she be isolated from her family. The doctor and Clara were afraid that Twain's constant talking would be more than Livy could take. A nurse was brought in to tend her, and Twain went around pinning notes on the trees asking the birds to sing softly.

"Our dear prisoner is where she is through over-work — day & night devotion to the children & me," he wrote. "We did not know how to value it. We know now."

It was October before Livy was able to return to Riverdale on a specially chartered coach, and once again Twain had to content himself with writing notes to her.

Not until December 30 was he able to see her, and he wrote in his notebook: "A splendid five minutes."

On February 2, 1903, their thirty-third wedding anniversary, he wrote: "It's a long time ago, my darling, but the 33 years have been richly profitable to us, through love — a love which has grown, not diminished, and is worth more each year than it was the year before. And so it will be always, dearest old Sweetheart of my youth."

Livy gradually improved, and the doctors said it would be good for her health if they moved to a milder climate. Mark and Livy decided to rent a villa in Florence, Italy, for the coming winter, but first they returned to Quarry Farm for the last time.

Livy spent much of her time outdoors in a wheelchair, and Mark wrote Twichell: "In the matter of superintending everything and everybody, [she] has resumed business at the old stand."

They moved to Florence in October 1903, and at first Livy was able to sit up an hour or two every day. But within two weeks after arriving, she suffered another heart attack. She was again confined

Mark and Livy in 1903. Twain wrote to her, "The 33 years have been richly profitable to us, through love."

to bed and Mark was not allowed to see her, but often he sat on the floor outside her door.

He began to spend much of his time reading or writing in bed, and Livy worried that this would weaken him. She had Clara read him a passage about the poet William Cullen Bryant, who still took vigorous, early-morning walks at the age of 80.

"Mr. Bryant was wonderful to do those early risings, and all that at eighty," Twain replied. "If ever I get to be eighty, I mean to do them, too."

He decided that Livy's best hope of improving would be for them to settle permanently in Florence, so he, Clara, and Jean looked at villas and at last they found a place they loved.

They hurried home to tell Livy about it and she "appeared better than she had for months," Clara said, "and was eager to hear every detail. . . . Then Jean and I left Father and Mother alone. It was now early in the evening. . . . "

Twain stayed with her an hour, then went to the parlor and sat at the piano. For the first time in years, he played and sang "the quaint negro hymns which no one cared for when I sang them, except Susy and her mother."

Twain said that once Susy died, "I could not put force and feeling into them without the inspiration of her approving presence. But now the force and feeling were all back, in full strength, and I was all alive, and it was as if eight years had fallen from me. In the midst of 'My Lord He call me! He call me by the thunder!' Jean crept into the room and sat down, to my astonishment and — embarrassment; and I stopped, but when she asked me to go on, only the astonishment remained. . . . "

Livy heard him and told Katy Leary, "He is singing a good-night carol for me."

Five minutes later, Mark Twain went into his wife's bedroom to say good night, and found Katy and the nurse supporting her. "I bent over her & looked in her face, & I think I spoke — I was surprised and troubled that she did not notice me. Then we understood, & our hearts broke."

Livy was dead, and he stayed by her side all night, caressing her hand. The next day he wrote Howells: "I am tired and old; I wish I were with Livy."

12

THIS VAST EMPTINESS

They buried Livy in Elmira beside Langdon and Susy. On her tombstone, Twain had engraved in the German language they both loved: *"Gott sei dir gnädig, O meine Wonne!"* — "God be gracious, Oh, my Bliss!"

Standing by the open grave, he vowed he would never watch another person he loved being lowered into the ground.

In the weeks that followed, said Katy Leary, "Mr. Clemens was just like a dead person. . . . But by and by they had to try to begin life again."

Clara suffered a nervous breakdown a few weeks later and entered a sanitarium. Then Jean broke several bones when a horse she was riding ran into a trolley car.

Twain warned Clara's doctor not to let her see any newspaper accounts of the accident, but then "performed one of his strange, unaccountable little acts," said Clara.

He hurried to see her "and, after a brief greeting, handed me a newspaper with the headlines: 'It is hoped that Mark Twain's youngest daughter, Jean, may live. Her horse fell on her and crushed her.'"

He then proceeded to give a hair-raising account of the accident, leaving Clara shaking her head and wondering "what kind of wheels were revolving in his mind, when his actions were so at variance with his intentions. But I never asked him."

In the fall, Mark and Jean moved to a house in New York City, where he lived in almost complete seclusion the first few months.

"Do try to reach through grief and feel the pressure of her hand," Helen Keller wrote him, "as I reach through darkness and feel the smile on my friends' lips and the light in their eyes though mine are closed."

Years before, he had written to Livy's sister: "I dreamed I was born & grew up & was a pilot on the Mississippi & a miner & a journalist in Nevada & a pilgrim in the Quaker City & had a wife & children & went to live in a villa at Florence — & this dream goes on & on & on & sometimes seems so real that I almost believe it is real. I wonder if it is."

Now his dreams began to haunt him, and he wondered more than ever what was real and what was not.

There was one dream where the audience at a lecture walked out because he could think of nothing to say, and another where poverty forced him "to go back to the river to earn a living. It is never a pleasant dream, either. . . . [usually] I am just about to start into a black shadow. . . . "

There were also dreams of racial violence. Even in sleep, he could not lose his obsession with poverty and race.

Twain wrote very little, but what he did write was powerful. His anger at injustice now reached a crescendo and was expressed in such writings as "The War Prayer" (a bitter attack on the "patriotism" that led Americans to support their government even when it waged war against innocent people), and "King Leopold's Soliloquy."

"I have told the truth in that," he said in putting "The War Prayer" aside, "and only dead men can tell the truth in this world. It can be published after I am dead."

"King Leopold's Soliloquy" was about Leopold II of Belgium, who had seized one million square miles in Africa and turned it into an incredibly brutal slave plantation that brought him millions. Powerful American financiers had just completed negotiations to share in the exploitation of the Congo.

No magazine in the United States would publish the article, so Twain gave it to the American Congo Reform Association to sell as a pamphlet "for the relief of the people of the Congo State."

As the months passed, Twain gradually began accepting invitations to banquets, where he was almost invariably asked to speak. He still felt lonely, though, and said he was "washing about in a forlorn sea of banquets & speechmaking."

Mark Twain in his well-known white suit, at home in Hartford, Connecticut.

It was also about this time that he started wearing white suits every day, because dark colors depressed him and light-colored clothing "enlivens the spirit."

"I go out very frequently and exhibit my clothes," he wrote Clara. "Howells has dubbed me the 'Whited Sepulchre.' Yes, dear child, I'm a 'recognized immortal genius' and a most dissipated one too."

Clara said at first people were "a bit startled at this apparition," but soon felt "nothing but emotional pleasure in the sight . . . "

Reporters and admirers streamed to visit him, and he was so well-known that people applauded when he entered a theater or restaurant. On December 5, 1905, the leading authors and editors of the day attended a banquet in honor of his seventieth birthday. One of the guests was Charles W. Chesnutt, a black novelist Twain had befriended.

Watching her father run up and down the stairs earlier in the day, Clara thought he was "younger now than I have ever felt."

His speech at the banquet, which was also attended by Howells, Twichell, and Henry Rogers, was about reaching the age of 70, "the Scriptural statute of limitations."

Twain said that now he had arrived "at pier No. 70," he wanted only to "nestle in the chimney corner, and smoke my pipe, and take my rest . . . "

He didn't seem quite ready to nestle, smoke, and rest yet, however. One night he attended a big supper and ball at midnight "and enjoyed it thoroughly till 4:05 A.M. when I came away with the last of the rioters."

He was still as impressed as ever by inventions, and often amused himself by playing an Aeolian Orchestrelle — a player piano.

He was also aware that formidable new weapons were being invented to wage war, and strongly disagreed with people who thought men would stop waging war rather than use these weapons.

"Man was created a bloody animal and I think he will always thirst for blood and will manage to have it," he told Jean.

The contradictions that had marked his life from the time he was a youth were more powerful than ever.

He said he abhorred violence, but he advocated violent revolution as the most effective way to end injustice, and declared that every right he enjoyed "was bought for me by rivers of blood."

He warned that this country was headed toward a dictatorship of the wealthy, and that only a strong labor movement could save democracy, yet he was proud of his friendship with some of the men most strongly opposed to labor.

He questioned the existence of a personal God, as he had throughout his life, but spent more time than ever demanding that He justify His actions.

In what critics would later call his "dark writings" — such as the short story "The Mysterious Stranger" and the essay, "What Is Man?" — he played with the theme of dream and reality that had fascinated him so long, and poured out his feelings about life.

Yet even in the midst of attacking man's brutality and folly, Twain also reaffirmed his belief that there was still hope for man because he possessed "one really effective weapon — laughter."

He added "The Mysterious Stranger" to the growing pile of manuscripts in his trunk, and it was not published until six years after his death.

"Don't part with your illusions," he had written a decade earlier in *Following the Equator*. "When they are gone you may still exist but you have ceased to live."

Now his illusions were gone, and he was a deeply lonely man. Often he purposely walked down Fifth Avenue as church was letting out, so the crowds would stare at him and greet him.

Once Howells, embarrassed by Twain's white clothes, tried to sneak him into a large dining room through a side entrance. Twain suddenly realized what he was doing and asked, "Isn't there another entrance to this place?"

When Howells admitted there was, Twain insisted on going downstairs to the lobby, then back upstairs to the dining room's main entrance so he could enjoy the crowd's recognition.

He had now reached "the grandpapa stage of life," but had no grandchildren. He must have felt this absence deeply, for he formed friendships with many children and loved to take them driving or visiting with him. Joe Twichell came down many weekends in an effort to relieve Twain's loneliness, but despite all these activities, loneliness seemed to be his constant companion.

Twain had begun writing his autobiography in the early 1870s, but set it aside. Now he knew his time was growing short, and when Albert Bigelow Paine asked if he could be his official biographer, Twain agreed.

He told Howells the autobiography "would live a couple of thousand years without any effort and would then take a fresh start and live the rest of the time."

Paine hired a stenographer, and Twain began dictating the book in January 1906. He did most of his talking in bed while propped against pillows and smoking cigars, with a jumble of papers scattered around him.

The book became a fascinating mixture of fact and fantasy, with Twain often unable to tell whether he was relating something that happened or something he just imagined.

"I don't believe these details are right," he said once, "but I don't care a rap. They will do just as well as the facts."

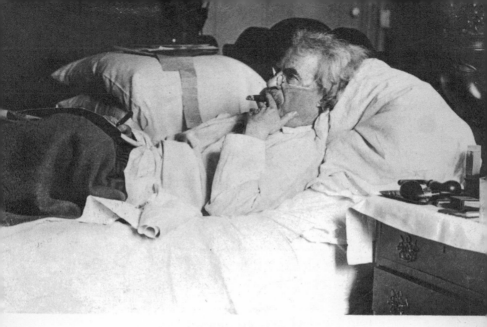

Mark Twain at work.

Paine's presence helped ease Twain's loneliness, and they often walked fifty blocks up to Central Park or played billiards till the early hours of the morning.

In the spring of 1907, Twain received word that Oxford University wanted to give him an honorary degree. He was delighted.

"Although I wouldn't cross an ocean again for the price of the ship that carried me, I am glad to do it for an Oxford degree," he wrote a friend in London.

His trip to England marked the climax of the public honors in his life and he relished the acclaim, starting with the stevedores cheering him as he left the ship.

Ever irreverent Twain, in Oxford robes and nightgown, 1908.

When he received his degree, dressed proudly in the university's scarlet and gray robe, "a veritable cyclone" of applause broke out.

Four weeks of whirlwind activity followed before he came back to the United States and loneliness. In the summer, Twain suffered severe heart pains while returning from the funeral of his nephew, Samuel Moffett.

"I came back here in bad shape . . . but I am all right again," he wrote Livy's sister. " . . . O fortunate Sam Moffett! fortunate Livy Clemens! doubly fortunate Susy! . . . there is never a moment that I am not glad, for the sake of the dead, that they have escaped."

Paine lived near Redding, Connecticut, and when he suggested that Twain buy some nearby land and build a house, Twain readily agreed.

He purchased 200 acres atop a hill, and hired Howells' architect son to design the house. His only requirements were that it have a large billiard room decorated in red, a living room large enough to hold his Orchestrelle, and several guest rooms.

"I don't want to see it, until the cat is purring on the hearth," he said.

Almost forty years before, Twain had written but never published a small book he called *Captain Stormfield's Visit to Heaven*. It was based on a dream related to him by his old friend, Captain Ned Wakeman, and told about an infinite number of heavens instead of just one.

Twain decided to publish his book in serial form in *Harper's Magazine* in 1907–8. He had tentatively named his new house "Innocence at Home," but decided to call it "Stormfield" because the money from *Harper's* helped pay for its construction and because "it is set so high that all the storms that come will beat upon it . . . "

In June 1908, he traveled to Redding to move into Stormfield, the first home of his own in seventeen years. A huge crowd met him at the station and he was escorted to the house in a carriage decorated with flowers. Then he was treated to a dinner party, fireworks, and a round of billiards.

Three months after moving in, burglars stole the family silverware but were caught the next day in a shootout with police. Twain promptly tacked a notice on his front door:

"To The next Burglar. There is nothing but plated ware in this house, now and henceforth. You will find it in that brass thing in the dining-room over in the corner by the basket of kittens. If you want the basket, put the kittens in the brass thing. . . . "

Jean was in a sanitarium at this time trying to find a cure for her epilepsy, and Clara was often away pursuing the concert singing career she had trained for in Vienna, so the family life Twain had dreamed of reestablishing at Stormfield was still a dream.

When Clara was home, however, she noticed that Twain was now greatly interested in reading about the stars and planets.

Once, while trying to calculate how long it took for light from certain stars to reach the earth, he said to Paine: "I came in with Halley's comet in 1835. It is coming again next year, and I expect to go out with it. . . . The Almighty has said, no doubt: 'Now here are these unaccountable freaks; they came in together, they must go out together.' Oh! I am looking forward to that."

In the spring of 1909, Jean finally came home. She seemed to be cured, and the next few months were happy ones.

"How eloquently glad and grateful she was to

cross her father's threshold again!" Twain said.

In the fall, Clara married Ossip Gabrilowitsch, a pianist she had met in Vienna. Twichell officiated at the ceremonies, with Twain dressed proudly in his Oxford robe. Jean was her sister's maid of honor and Clara said "everyone was in bright spirits, like the October day that blazed brilliant in resplendent autumn colors."

Clara's wedding photo. Left to right: Mark Twain, Charles Langdon, Jean Clemens, Ossip Gabrilowitsch (the groom), Clara Clemens Gabrilowitsch, and Joseph Twichell.

In his congratulations to his daughter and new son-in-law, Twain said the marriage pleased him, but added: "I grieve for you. Not for both of you . . . but for the one that is fated to be left behind."

Clara and Ossip went to Europe to live, and Twain said her departure "was hard, but I could bear it, for I had Jean left. I said *we* would be a family. We said we would be close comrades and happy — just we two."

In November, Twain traveled to Bermuda with Paine, but returned to Stormfield to spend Christmas with Jean. Though she had not suffered a seizure in months, he worried about how hard she was driving herself, and tried to get her to slow down.

"The matter ended in a compromise," he remembered afterwards. "I submitted. I always did."

On the evening of December 23, they had dinner together and then "strolled hand in hand . . . and sat down in the library and chatted and planned and discussed, cheerily and happily . . . then went upstairs, Jean's friendly German dog following."

When Jean told her father she couldn't kiss him good night because she had a cold, "I bent and kissed her hand. She was moved — I saw it in her eyes — and she impulsively kissed my hand in return. Then . . . we parted."

The next morning, Katy Leary hurried into his

room, stood trembling at his bedside, and said: *"Miss Jean is dead!"*

Jean had drowned after suffering an epileptic seizure in the bathtub.

"Possibly I know now what the soldier feels when a bullet crashes through his heart," Twain told Paine.

Clinging to his vow never to see another person he loved lowered into a grave, he refused to accompany her body to Elmira and see her buried in the plot with her mother, sister, and brother.

Instead, Katy Leary made the trip while Twain watched them leave the house during a soft, heavy snowstorm. He stayed upstairs, said Clara, "watching Jean going away from him for the last time."

Twain said that if he knew the word that could call Jean back to life, "I would beg for strength to withhold the word. And I would have the strength. . . . "

For most of the next two days, while a blizzard raged over the house, he tried to find peace by writing down everything he remembered about Jean — the daughter who had now received "that gift which makes all other gifts mean and poor — death."

He wrote Clara that for several months, he had been in great distress because he realized "no one stood between her and danger but me — and I could die at any moment, and then — oh then what would become of her!"

He had made a will several months earlier, divid-

ing his copyrights and other property evenly between Clara and Jean. But he thought the books
would soon be worth little or nothing, and bring in
too little income for his daughters to live on. Now he
no longer had to worry about Jean.

He let his mind roam back to happier days and
saw his children "romp again with George — that
peerless black ex-slave and children's idol who came
one day — a flitting stranger — to wash windows
and stayed eighteen years."

Howells came for several days, and said that every
morning "I heard him sounding my name through
the house, for the fun of it . . . and if I looked out of
my door, there he was in his long nightgown sway-
ing up and down the corridor, and wagging his
great, white head like a boy that leaves his bed and
comes out in the hope of frolic with some one."

And once again, Twain sought solace in the spirituals that touched the deepest part of him, singing
them to Howells in a "quavering tenor" filled with
fervor and passion.

But he could not stand the emptiness and desolation of Stormfield, and called himself a fool for having built it.

"Why did I build this house two years ago?" he
asked bitterly. "To shelter this vast emptiness?"

Less than two weeks after Jean's death, he sailed
to Bermuda, planning to stay all winter in the
warmth and sunshine. At first he felt well enough to

Mark Twain on the beach in Bermuda in 1908.

go on picnics, play miniature golf, and enjoy swimming and boating.

"Good time, good home, tranquil contentment all day and every day," he wrote Paine.

Strangers concerned about reports of his health sent him remedies, and he thanked them with a form letter: "Dear Sir (or Madam)," it read. "I try every remedy sent to me. I am now on No. 67. Yours is 2,653. I am looking forward to its beneficial results."

But the pains in his heart grew worse, and he made plans to return home.

"I don't want to die here," he said, "for this is an unkind place for a person in that condition. I should have to lie in the undertaker's cellar until the ship would remove me and it is dark down there and unpleasant. . . . I don't want to die there. I am growing more and more particular about the place."

Paine hurried to Bermuda to bring him home, and they started back on April 12, 1910. Twain could hardly breathe, and once he asked Paine if there wasn't some way "to resign" from life.

"I am like a bird in a cage," he said, "always expecting to get out, and always beaten back by the wires. . . . "

He arrived at Stormfield a few days before Clara came from Germany. She said her father "was pathetically anxious to inform me about the financial state of affairs. . . . He appeared skeptical . . . as to whether the sale of his books would continue for more than a brief period after his death."

One day Paine, who spent much of his time sitting by Twain's bedside, carried a message to Clara saying her father wanted her to sing some Scotch songs he always liked. At first she doubted if she had the emotional strength to sing for him, but finally managed.

On the morning of the twenty-first, he suddenly opened his eyes and said to her: "Goodbye dear, if we meet — "

Then he sunk into a coma and died that evening, said Clara, as "Halley's comet was once more shining in the sky, as it had done at his birth."

His funeral was held in Brick Church in New York City, and thousands came to say good-bye.

Joe Twichell lifted his voice "in the prayer which he wailed through in broken-hearted supplication" for his friend of forty years, and then Howells came to say his last good-bye.

"I looked a moment at the face I knew so well," he said, "and it was patient with the patience I had so

Twain's funeral in New York City in 1910.

often seen in it: something of a puzzle, a great silent dignity, an assent to what must be from the depths of a nature whose tragical seriousness broke in the laughter which the unwise took for the whole of him.

"Emerson, Longfellow, Lowell, Holmes — I knew them all and all the rest of our sages, poets, seers, critics, humorists; they were like one another and like other literary men; but Clemens was sole, incomparable, the Lincoln of our literature."

" **M**y books are water; those of the great geniuses are wine. Everybody drinks water."
Mark Twain

Many scholars and critics have disagreed with Howell's glowing analysis of Mark Twain's talent, but his books continue to be among the most popular ever written.

Yet the fact remains that Mark Twain is still thought of primarily as a humorist or a writer of children's books, as if the man who wrote *The Celebrated Jumping Frog of Calaveras County*, *The Adventures of Tom Sawyer*, and *The Adventures of Huckleberry Finn* did not also write *The Mysterious Stranger*, *King Leopold's Soliloquy*, and *The United States of Lyncherdom*.

People who feel comfortable with his image as a kindly old man in white clothes telling funny stories, do not feel comfortable with his image as an angry man denouncing racism, unethical business practices, blind patriotism, or the exploitation of the poor.

His writing was a mirror that reflected his life and

the life of the society that helped shape him. And as he matured, he grew increasingly critical and fearful about the issue that had troubled his sleep even as a child: racism and the violence that flowed from it.

Like generations of Americans before and since, the seeds of racism were planted in him as a child. And though he didn't always succeed in overcoming that bitter heritage (privately using the word "nigger," for instance, throughout his life), few people have tried harder or been more fearful of the consequences of failure — for himself and for his country.

More than fifty years after seeing a black man murdered by his owner on a street in Hannibal, Mark Twain made a note to use such an episode in a story that involved the lynching of an innocent black woman. The idyllic Southern images that had once filled his writing, turned increasingly into nightmarish images haunted by race and racism.

In his last long piece of fiction about the South, "Which Was It?," Hannibal had turned into a bleak, snowbound Indiantown haunted by the spectre of racial revenge from a man whose father was a wealthy white aristocrat, and whose mother was a black slave.

The racial harmony Twain had envisioned with Jim and Huck on the raft so many years before had given way to a future filled with racial hatred. And he often seemed to identify more strongly with black

Americans and other people of color than he identified with whites.

It is ironic that Mark Twain has been attacked as an anti-black racist, primarily because of his writings in *Huckleberry Finn*. There *is* much that is objectionable in the book, including the unlikely ending where whites decide to give Jim his freedom. The ending effectively says that only whites control black destiny, and it doesn't really matter what black people do to try and control their own lives.

Jim is also full of superstitions, a dialect that sounds more like that of a minstrel than a real man, and often comes across as a stereotype rather than a fully developed human being.

Mark Twain's frequent use of the word "nigger" is also offensive, especially to black students in mixed classrooms (though much of the objection to teaching *Huckleberry Finn* could be overcome if more was taught about Twain's racial beliefs and the conditions he was attacking).

When all is said and done, however, *Huckleberry Finn* is a book that denounced racial injustice, showed that black people valued freedom as much as white people, and would fight as hard to achieve it.

There would be no *Huckleberry Finn* if Mark Twain had not possessed the desire to show, however inadequately at times, that a black man was as fully human as any other man. There would be no *Huckleberry Finn* if Mark Twain had not possessed the desire to destroy the mythology that justified white supremacy, with all its violence and injustice.

Mark Twain looked at the world around him, and used the language he helped create to write "sermons" about that world.

"I have always preached," he said in summing up his career. "That is the reason I have lasted thirty years. If the humor came of its own accord and uninvited I have allowed it a place in my sermon, but I was not writing the sermon for the sake of the humor. I should have written the sermon just the same, whether any humor applied for admission or not."

He was like some fiery prophet from the Bible he claimed not to believe in, railing against injustice wherever he found it, then suddenly stopping to tell a joke.

The folly of people angered him so because he loved them so, and he felt frustrated because there was always so much more he wanted to say.

He had expressed the frustration to Howells years before, after completing *A Connecticut Yankee*, and the words summed up his life as a writer and a man:

"Well, my book is written — let it go. But if it were only to write over again there wouldn't be so many things left out. They burn in me; and they keep multiplying and multiplying; but now they can't ever be said."

BIBLIOGRAPHY

Anderson, Frederick; Frank, Michael B.; and Sanderson, Kenneth M.; eds. *Mark Twain's Notebooks & Journals*. Vol. 1 (1855–1873). Berkeley: University of California Press, 1975.

Anderson, Frederick; Salamo, Lin; and Stein, Bernard L.; eds. *Mark Twain's Notebooks & Journals*. Vol. 2 (1877–1883). The Mark Twain Papers. Berkeley: University of California Press, 1975.

Anderson, Frederick, ed. *A Pen Warmed Up in Hell: Mark Twain in Protest*. New York: Harper & Row, 1979.

Ayres, Alex, ed. *The Wit and Wisdom of Mark Twain*. New York: Harper & Row, 1987.

Branch, Edgar Marquess; Frank, Michael B.; and Sanderson, Kenneth M.; eds. *Mark Twain's Letters, Vol. 1: 1853–1866*. Berkeley: University of California Press, 1988.

Branch, Edgar Marquess, and Hirst, Robert H., eds. *The Works of Mark Twain, Vol. 1: Early Tales and Sketches (1851–1864)*. Berkeley: University of California Press, 1979.

Brooks, Van Wyck. *The Ordeal of Mark Twain*. New York: E.P. Cutton & Company, 1933.

Browning, Robert Pack; Frank, Michael B.; and Salamo, Lin; eds. *Mark Twain's Notebooks and Journals. Vol. 3 (1883–1891)*. Berkeley: University of California Press, 1979.

Clemens, Clara. *My Father, Mark Twain*. New York: Harper & Brothers, 1931.

Clemens, Susy. *Papa: An Intimate Biography*, ed. Charles Neider. Garden City: Doubleday, 1985.

DeVoto, Bernard, ed. *Mark Twain in Eruption*. New York: Harper & Brothers, 1940.

———. *Mark Twain's America*. Boston: Houghton Mifflin Co., 1951.

———, ed. *Letters From the Earth*. New York: Harper-Perennial, 1991.

Duskis, Henry, ed. *The Forgotten Writings of Mark Twain*. New York: Philosophical Library, 1963.

Fischer, Victor, and Frank, Michael B., eds. *Mark Twain's Letters, Vol. 3: 1869*. Berkeley: University of California Press, 1992.

Fishkin, Shelley Fisher. *Was Huck Black? Mark Twain and African American Voices*. New York: Oxford University Press, 1993.

Foner, Phillip. *Mark Twain: Social Critic*. New York: International Publishers, 1972.

Geismar, Maxwell. *Mark Twain: An American Prophet*. Boston: Houghton Mifflin, 1970.

———, ed. *Mark Twain & the Three R's: Race, Religion, Revolution and Related Matters*. New York: Bobbs-Merrill, 1973.

Hill, Hamlin, ed. *Mark Twain's Letters to His Publishers, 1867–1894*. Berkeley: University of California Press, 1967.

Howells, William Dean. *My Mark Twain*. New York: Harper & Brothers, 1910.

Kaplan, Justin. *Mr. Clemens and Mark Twain: A Biography*. New York: Touchstone, 1966.

Lauber, John. *The Inventions of Mark Twain*. New York: Harper & Collins, 1990.

Lawton, Mary. *A Lifetime With Mark Twain: The Memories of Katy Leary, for Thirty Years His Faithful and Devoted Servant*. New York: Harcourt, Brace and Co., 1925.

Meltzer, Milton, ed. *Mark Twain Himself*. New York: Wings Books, 1993.

Neider, Charles, ed. *The Complete Humorous Sketches and Tales of Mark Twain*. Garden City: Doubleday & Co., 1961.

——, ed. *The Autobiography of Mark Twain*. New York: HarperPerennial, 1959.

——, ed. *The Complete Short Stories of Mark Twain*. Garden City: Doubleday and Co., 1985.

Paine, Albert Bigelow, ed. *Mark Twain's Letters*. 2 vols. New York: Harper & Brothers, 1929.

——, ed. *Mark Twain's Notebook*. New York: Harper & Brothers, 1935.

——, ed. *Mark Twain's Autobiography*. 3 vols. New York: Harper & Brothers, 1912.

Pettit, Arthur. *Mark Twain & the South*. Lexington, Kentucky: University of Kentucky Press, 1974.

Sanborn, Margaret. *Mark Twain: The Bachelor Years*. Garden City: Doubleday, 1990.

Smith, Harriet Elinor, and Bucci, Richard, eds. *Mark Twain's Letters, Vol. 2: 1867–1868*. Berkeley: University of California Press, 1990.

Smith, Henry Nash, and Gibson, William M., eds. *Mark Twain—Howells Letters, 1872–1910*. 2 vols. Cambridge: Harvard University Press, 1960.

Smith, Henry Nash, ed. *Mark Twain of the Enterprise*. Berkeley: University of California Press, 1957.

Tuckey, John S., ed. *The Devil's Race-Track: Mark Twain's Great Dark Writings*. Berkeley: University of California Press, 1980.

———, ed. *Mark Twain's Which Was the Dream?* Berkeley: University of California Press, 1967.

Twain, Mark. *Adventures of Huckleberry Finn*. Berkeley: University of California Press, 1985.

———. *The Adventures of Tom Sawyer*. Berkeley: University of California Press, 1982.

———. *A Connecticut Yankee in King Arthur's Court*. Berkeley: University of California Press, 1983.

———. *Following the Equator*. New York: Harper & Brothers, 1925.

———. *The Innocents Abroad*. New York: New American Library, 1966.

———. *The Prince and the Pauper*. Berkeley: University of California Press, 1983.

———. *Roughing It*. Berkeley: University of California Press, 1972.

———. *Tom Sawyer Abroad/Tom Sawyer, Detective*. Berkeley: University of California Press, 1982.

Wagenknecht, Edward. *Mark Twain: The Man and His Work*. New Haven: Yale University Press, 1935.

Wecter, Dixon, ed. *The Love Letters of Mark Twain*. New York: Harper & Brothers, 1949.

Willis, Resa. *Mark and Livy: The Love Story of Mark Twain and the Woman Who Almost Tamed Him*. New York: Atheneum, 1992.

INDEX

Page references in italics indicate illustrations or photographs.